WATERBORNE WARRIORS

U.S. Army Riverine Craft in Vietnam

By John M. Carrico

SFC, U.S. Army (Retired)

*One of the things that we learned very quickly was by the use of boats
the enemy was not alert to our movement to combat."*
Brigadier General Fulton, circa 1967.

Waterborne Warriors
Copyright © 2011 by John M. Carrico.

Edited by Glenda A. Gill.

Library of Congress Control Number: 2011901276
ISBN-13: 978-0-9794231-3-0
ISBN-10:   0-9794231-3-9
First Edition Softcover

To order additional copies of this book, contact:
Brown Water Enterprises
www.brownwater.net

CONTENTS

INTRODUCTION AND DEDICATION

My first book, *Vietnam Ironclads*, was about the unique river assault craft operated by the U.S. Navy during the Vietnam War. While conducting research for *Vietnam Ironclads*, I was in contact with several veterans who asked me if I planned to write anything about the boats used by the U.S. Army in Vietnam. As a former soldier, naturally I was intrigued and wanted to learn more, so I decided to publish another photo history book. As I searched for information, I was amazed by how many different types of vessels the U.S. Army actually operated in Vietnam. For example, there were boats as large as the USNS Corpus Christy Bay, which was a floating helicopter repair ship. In addition, there were large and small tug boats, tankers, landing craft of various sizes, and small patrol boats. Oddly I discovered that very little has been published about Army watercraft. The sailors of the brown-water navy and their famous "plastic patrol boats" have been widely publicized in books, model kits and Hollywood films such as *Apocalypse Now*; but not much credit has been given to the soldier–mariners, who also served in Southeast Asia. Because of publishing constraints, I was forced to narrow the scope of this book and focus on Army boats that were used primarily for riverine warfare. I dedicate this book to all of the brave Waterborne Warriors who fought and lost their lives in the Republic of South Vietnam.

ACKNOWLEDGMENTS

I wish to thank the highly professional staff of the National Archives located at College Park, Maryland, and Rich Baker, Historian at the U.S. Army Military Historical Institute in Carlyle Barracks, Pennsylvania, for providing tremendous assistance with my research and locating hundreds of official Department of Defense (DoD) photographs for this book. I would also like to thank Jenifer Stepp, Assistant Editor to the Chief Operating Officer of *Stars & Stripes* for granting me permission to print an excellent wartime airboat photograph. Also I would like to thank Major (MAJ) Mandy MacWhirter for thinking of me and taking some excellent photographs of the Aircat airboat on display at the War Memorial of Korea. Thanks go to David Hanselman, Director of the U.S. Army Transportation Museum at Fort Eustis, Virginia, for allowing me to photograph the only remaining U.S. Army SK-5 Air-Cushion Vehicle (ACV). Thank you to James Burke for allowing me to join your Yahoo Group of former Army landing craft crewmen and sharing your wonderful stories with me. I also give thanks to the 458th "Sea Tigers" Veterans Group for allowing me to print several outstanding personal photographs of Army patrol boats in Vietnam. Heartfelt thanks goes to my editors, MAJ Glenda Gill and Inez Schonauer.

PICTURE CREDITS

Robert Brower

James Burke

Jim Bury

Mike Hebert

Mandy MacWhirter

Jerry McDevitt

Bruce McIlhaney Pacific Stars and Stripes

Arlyn Musselman

Angelo Rossetti

United States National Archives and Records Administration (NARA)

United States Army (U.S. Army)

U.S. Army Corps of Engineers

U.S. Army Military Historical Institute (USAMHI)

Don Valkie

Jerry Wallace

Thomas Wonsiewicz

Book cover: (front) Sergeant First Class (SFC) Robert Todd, Assistant Team Leader, Detachment A-404, Delta Company, the Special Forces Group (Airborne) mans an .30 Caliber Machine Gun mounted on the bow of an Aircat airboat while instructing a MIKE Force student on how to pilot the boat in 1970. (NARA); (back) A U.S. Army SK-5 Air-Cushion Vehicle effortlessly maneuvers over dry land during a search and destroy operation in 1968. (USAMHI)

The photograph of ACV-903 on display at Fort Eustis, Virginia, is provided by the author.

TERMINOLOGY

AACV	Assault Air-Cushion Vehicle
ABN	Airborne
ACTIVN	Army Concept Team in Vietnam
ACV	Air-Cushion Vehicle
Aft	Rear or after section of a boat
AGL	Automatic Grenade Launcher
Aircat	Hurricane Airboat
AMMI	Navy construction pontoon
AN/ARC	Army-Navy/Aircraft Radio Communications
AN/PRC	Army-Navy/Portable Radio Communications
AN/MRC	Army-Navy/Mobile Radio Communications
AN/VRC	Army-Navy/Vehicular Radio Communications
APC	Armored Personnel Carrier
ATC	Armored Troop Carrier, a Navy LCM(6) landing craft conversion
ARVN	Army of the Republic of Vietnam
AVGAS	Aviation Gasoline
BEB	Bridge Erection Boat
BDE	Brigade
BN	Battalion
BW	Boston Whaler, a small fiberglass boat powered by an outboard motor
Bow	Front of a boat
CDR	Commander
CO	Company
COMUSMACV	Commander, United States Military Assistance Command Vietnam
CP	Command Post
CTZ	Corps Tactical Zone
Decca	A British company that produced a low-frequency navigational radar system
DIV	Division
EAB	Engineer Assault Boat
ENSURE	Expedited Non-Standard Urgent Requirement for Equipment Program
FDC	Fire Direction Center
FM	Frequency Modulated Radio System
FS	Federal Standard, a color system developed by the U.S. government
GE	General Electric
GL	Grenade Launcher
GM	General Motors
Hp	Horsepower
Hootch	Makeshift dwelling
ID	Infantry Division
In country	Slang used to describe the Vietnam-theater of operations
KSB	Kenner Ski Barge
LARC-V	Lighter, Amphibious, Resupply, Cargo-vehicle (5-ton)
LCM	Landing Craft Mechanized
LCVP	Landing Craft Vehicle, Personnel

LIB	Light Infantry Brigade
LRRP	Long Range Reconnaissance Patrol
LST	Landing Ship, Tank
LZ	Landing Zone
MACV	Military Assistance Command Vietnam
MB	Medium Boat
MBP	Motor Boat Plastic
MG	Machine gun
Mike Boat	Nickname for the Army Landing Craft Mechanized, Mark-8
MOGAS	Motor Gasoline
Monitor	Heavily armed naval vessel that supported the ATCs and assault troops
Monster	Nickname given to Air-Cushion Vehicles
MP	Military Police
MPD	Mobile Personnel Detector or "People Sniffer"
MPH	Miles per hour
MRF	Mobile Riverine Force (forces organized to conduct riverine operations)
NIOTC	Naval Inshore Operations Training Center
NOR	Not Operationally Ready, also means Non-Mission Capable (NMC)
NSA	Naval Support Activity
Outport	A detachment of boats from the 458th TC (PBR), who guarded Army seaports
PAB	Plastic Assault Boat
PACV	Patrol Air-Cushion Vehicle
PBR	Patrol Boat River
Port	Left side of a boat when standing on the deck facing forward
PPI	Plan Position Indicator
RAC	River Assault Craft
RAG	River Assault Group
Riverine Warfare	Combat and associated support operations in a riverine environment
R.O.K.	Republic of Korea
RPC	River Patrol Craft
RPG	Rocket Propelled Grenade, an enemy shoulder-fired anti-tank weapon
RSSZ	Rung Sat Special Zone
RVN	Republic of Vietnam
Screw	Boat propeller
SF	Special Forces
Skimmer	Airboat tested in Vietnam, also a nickname used for the Boston Whaler
Skycrane	CH-54 Tarhe Helicopter
SOP	Standard Operating Procedures
SSB	Swimmer Support Boat, also called the Dong Nai by the Vietnamese
Starboard	Right side of a boat when standing on the deck facing forward
TC	Transportation Company
TM	Technical Manual
VC	Viet Cong
VHF	Very High Frequency (radio system)
Waterborne	Combat and support forces who move around the battlefield in watercraft
Well Deck	Cargo area or troop compartment of the LCM
XM	Experimental Model of a weapon system
Yaw	The ability of a vehicle to rotate from left to right

Chapter One

ARMY RIVERINE OPERATIONS

In May 1965, the first major U.S. Army ground combat units were deployed to the Republic of Vietnam (RVN), which is one of the most austere areas in the world. Here the Army faced two enemies–the Viet Cong (VC) and the terrain.[1] Vietnam is a country of extremes. In the north and central highlands are tropical jungles and mountains. The south is flat with countless waterways and mangrove forests. The southern Mekong Delta Region is a maze of flooded rice paddies that restricted ordinary ground movement and presented a challenge for anyone fighting there. New techniques and American ingenuity was needed to overcome the harsh operating conditions. As a result, the U.S. military launched a comprehensive effort to negotiate the rivers and swamps.

Combat operations in a riverine environment require special planning and tactics. In the early 1960's, the U.S. Army was not trained or equipped to fight on inundated terrain. The last time the military was heavily involved in riverine warfare was during the American Civil War. The tactics developed over 100 years earlier while fighting on the Mississippi River could be used to control Vietnam's inland waterways and deny the enemy safe areas from which to launch attacks. This type of warfare would demand the use of combat forces that could rapidly move across the battlefield in specially designed watercraft.

Two soldiers of the 9th Infantry Division (ID) struggle through the Mekong Delta mud in 1968. Field conditions like this necessitated the creation of specialized vehicles that could easily glide over water, rice paddies, and dry land. The solution was the tactical employment of commercial airboats and hovercraft by the U.S. Army. (USAMHI)

(left) Keeping soldiers dry and their gear functioning properly in a tropical environment was a serious challenge confronted by the Army in Vietnam. Great steps were taken to provide innovative weapons and equipment to improve the basic infantryman's fighting capabilities in this harsh terrain. Soldiers rode in specially designed watercraft and were given experimental clothing like mesh jungle boots, bivouac slippers, and waterproof socks. The soldiers also had to rely on individual field expedient methods to keep items from getting wet like placing a change of socks, cigarettes, and matches high and dry on their helmets using elastic bands. (USAMHI)

An infantryman takes cover in a flooded ditch beneath a makeshift palm tree bridge. A soldier's combat effectiveness diminished significantly after 48-hours of constant exposure to water in the swamps. Skin disease of the feet reduced the combat strength of a unit by 35% after 72 hours and 50% after 96 hours of exposure. The 9th ID adopted a 24-hour drying out period after 48-hours of continuous exposure to water.[2] (USAMHI)

Most people think the U.S. Navy is the only branch of service that operates military watercraft. This is simply not true. Since the American Revolution, the U.S. Army has had its own fleet of boats. The U.S. Navy was originally formed in 1775 to conduct blue-water operations. It wasn't until 1812, during the Great Lakes Campaign of the American Civil War, when the Navy took over Brown Water Riverine Operations from the Army. However, the Navy only wanted boats with guns and not the Army's "ash & trash" haulers–the Navy had little interest in unarmed transportation vessels. Ironically, in 1898 during the Spanish-American War, the Army had to purchase its own troop ships to deploy soldiers to Cuba and to the Philippines. The Army couldn't completely depend on the Navy to meet its mobility needs, so the Army Transportation Service was created and was operational until 1942 when it became part of the U.S. Army Transportation Corps.[3]

It's also a little known fact that during World War II (WWII), and throughout the Korean War, the vast majority of landing craft belonged to the Army–not the Navy. Since the end of WWII, the United States was prepared for WWIII against the Soviet Union in Europe. Thankfully, WWIII never materialized and the resulting Cold War inadvertently prepared the U.S. military for combat in Southeast Asia. New technologies in amphibious warfare were being developed to engage large conventional armies. Some of this equipment could be adapted to fight a counterinsurgency against small guerrilla forces in South Vietnam. The Mekong Delta was an ideal location for the testing and employment of specialized riverine craft because most of the countryside was covered by water.[4]

Movement by foot in the Mekong Delta was an exhausting task. The VC placed mines and booby traps on the rice paddy dikes so the infantrymen had little choice but to struggle through the flooded countryside. Most wheeled vehicles were restricted to the few existing solid-road networks in Vietnam. Tracked vehicles, like the Armored Personnel Carrier (APC), could cross-flooded rice paddies with relative ease but tanks were so heavy that they sank or became stuck in the mud. The Army did not have any specialized amphibious tanks, so the employment of the Armored Fighting Vehicle (AFV) in the Mekong Delta was considered largely ineffective.[5]

Communications and rapid mobility were essential to win battles in the RVN. The M-113 APC in the background was amphibious, but boats were a more practical mode of transportation in the Mekong Delta. (NARA)

The Marsh Screw Amphibian was developed by the Chrysler Corporation in 1963 to satisfy an urgent need for a simplified, mobile surface vehicle that could traverse all types of terrain in riverine areas, such as rice paddies, marshes and swamps, weed-clogged waterways, mud banks, and hard surfaces. The development of the Marsh Screw was based on the principle of the 3rd Century B.C. Archimedes' screw, which was adapted for use in water and soft soil. The Marsh Screw was ultimately rejected by the Army because of disappointing test results on soft soil, particularly sand.[6] (U.S. Army Corps of Engineers)

Soldiers of the 9th ID load Navy Armored Troop Carriers (ATC) from the barracks ship, *USS Benewah*, in preparation for a MRF operation in 1967. The Landing Craft Mechanized, Mark-6 [LCM(6)] formed the basis for the Navy RAC Modification Program. The specially designed RAC had steel bars and armor plates added to protect the assault troops and crewmembers from small arms fire and shrapnel. (USAMHI)

A map of South Vietnam's Corps Tactical Zones (CTZ), also called Military Regions. South Vietnam was subdivided into four geographical CTZs (I–IV). The Mekong Delta encompassed IV CTZ and the lower portion of III CTZ south of the capital Saigon. The 9th ID Area of Operations (AO) was the entire Mekong Delta. (U.S. Army)

One solution to facilitate movement in the Mekong Delta was to create a joint Mobile Riverine Force (MRF) by combining Army infantry and artillery elements with a naval assault flotilla. The Navy modified two hundred shallow draft landing craft with extra weapons and armor, calling them River Assault Craft (RAC). However, when forming the MRF, the Navy had no desire to handle logistical support, so the Navy provided gunboats, and Army landing craft were used to haul the "beans & bullets."[7] There is a popular saying that the U.S. Army has more boats than the U.S. Navy. While the statement is not true, the Army operated hundreds of vessels and sent many "soldier-mariners" to Vietnam. Army watercraft provided a necessary capability, and filled the void where Navy assets were unavailable to support.

Three Army infantry brigades were tasked to conduct riverine combat operations in Vietnam. The Navy's RAC only supported two brigades from the 9th ID in the Mekong Delta. The 199th Light Infantry Brigade (LIB) operating in the northern Mekong Delta Region of III Corps Tactical Zone (CTZ) was provided landing craft support by the Army's 1099th Medium Boat Company. The Army had three medium boat companies hauling troops and supplies up and down the rivers of III and IV CTZ. In addition, the Army had another medium boat company attached to the 9th ID to provide waterborne artillery support.[8] Combined Army/Navy Riverine Operations began in early 1967 using the thousands of Mekong Delta waterways as a giant highway. The MRF attacked isolated areas where enemy troops had once operated undetected for years. These operations were very effective, but soldiers

Soldiers of the 199th LIB disembark from a Vietnamese LCM(6) into the Rung Sat Special Zone (RSSZ) in 1968. The Army's 199th LIB operated its on miniature MRF in conjunction with the South Vietnamese River Assault Group (RAG) 27. The Force typically used one Vietnamese monitor, one Command Boat, six–to–eight Vietnamese River Patrol Craft (RPC), four–to–six Vietnamese LCM(6), and two U.S. Army LCM(8).[10] (USAMHI)

could only fight in this environment for a few days at a time because of foot injuries caused by extended exposure to water.[9]

The VC moved primarily by sampan in the Mekong Delta, so trudging through mangrove swamps to outmaneuver an enemy who sought to avoid contact was sometimes futile. South Vietnamese Forces were using four types of boats in the Mekong Delta: the Landing Craft Vehicle, Personnel (LCVP); the 14-foot Plastic Assault Boat (PAB); the Dong Nai Swimmer Support Boat (SSB); and the Sampan. These boats were generally slow and could not pursue VC sampans in low water with heavy aquatic growth, which fouled propellers.[11] In order for the U.S. Army to fight more effectively in this difficult terrain, specialized combat watercraft needed to be developed. To meet the challenge, the Army searched the commercial boat industry and transformed civilian hovercraft, airboats, ski-boats, barges, and fiberglass pleasure craft into revolutionary fighting machines.

The Dong Nai SSB was used primarily by South Vietnamese Forces operating in the Mekong Delta early in the war. The SSB was 14 feet long, weighed 375 pounds, and was constructed of bonded polystyrofoam planks covered with fiberglass. The boat didn't handle very well in choppy water and it was powered by a 25-hp or 40-hp outboard motor, which only achieved a maximum of 17 miles per hour (MPR) when the boat was fully loaded with troops. A logical replacement for the SSB was the American made Boston Whaler or Kenner Ski Barge.[12] (NARA)

A South Vietnamese RPC from RAG 30 carries "Redcatchers" of the 199th LIB across a river during riverine operations south of Saigon on 5 July 1968. (USAMHI)

A modified South Vietnamese LCM(6) "RAGBOAT" transports U.S. Army Soldiers during a river assault operation near Saigon in 1968. Notice the modified gun turrets on the stern and makeshift tarp added over the well deck to provide the soldiers some relief from the blazing sun. (USAMHI)

Riverine Infantrymen disembark from Navy RAC in the Mekong Delta circa 1968. The maneuver element of the MRF was assigned to the 9th ID, who had no specialized training in riverine warfare before they deployed to Vietnam. As the war progressed, the MRF became an effective fighting force using tactics that were originally developed during the American Civil War. (USAMHI)

A South Vietnamese LCM Command Boat of RAG 27 is nosed into a shoreline. Soldiers of the 199th LIB prepare to dismount to conduct a foot patrol in 1968. (USAMHI)

A U.S. Army Patrol Boat River (PBR) Mark (MK) 2 from the 458th Transportation Company (TC) patrols a waterway in South Vietnam. The PBR was a 32-foot fiberglass patrol craft that was adapted from a commercial pleasure boat built by the Uniflite Corporation. Army PBRs had awesome firepower, were extremely maneuverable and could reach speeds over 30 MPR.[13] (U.S. Army)

Army Reconnaissance Soldiers from the 25th ID move toward a South Vietnamese LCM(6) for extraction in August 1970. These modified boats were sometimes referred to as "long" or "heavy" LCMs. Notice the two PBRs tied-up to the landing craft. (NARA)

The tactical employment of helicopters was particularly successful when combined with waterborne operations by enveloping the enemy from the air and ground, simultaneously. (USAMHI)

The helicopter also played a vital role in riverine operations. They were used to deliver combat troops, heavy artillery, and vital supplies rapidly into battle. This was especially important in the Mekong Delta, where overland movement was arduous and time consuming. Helicopters were used to lift troops directly from their base camps straight into landing zones (LZ) located near the enemy. The LZs were usually nothing more than flooded rice paddies, so helicopters would descend very low and the troops would jump from the hovering aircraft. Normally, when an operation was completed, the soldiers would be extracted by boat and transported back to their bases to recuperate.[14]

Traveling over water is the Army's primary mode of transportation in a riverine environment. Foot marches were the least desirable way for maneuvering ground forces because it severely limited a unit's rate of travel. The most preferred method was a combination of all available means of mobility–foot, wheeled or tracked vehicles, boats, and helicopters. Exploiting the movement, fire support, and logistical assets significantly enhanced the Army's firepower and maneuver capabilities in the Mekong Delta. Vietnam was an ideal war for the employment of riverine craft.[15]

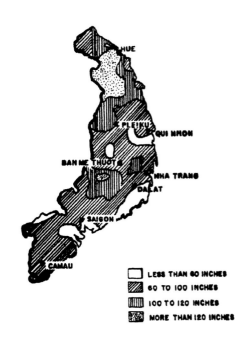

	LESS THAN 60 INCHES
	60 TO 100 INCHES
	100 TO 120 INCHES
	MORE THAN 120 INCHES

The average annual precipitation for South Vietnam. The Mekong Delta Region would generally receive between five and eight-feet of rain annually, in an area that was already mostly submerged by water. (U.S. Army)

17

Soldiers of the 199th LIB relax in the well deck of a South Vietnamese operated LCM(6) in 1968. Because the 199th used unmodified landing craft, two platoons–roughly 80 soldiers, could be transported in one LCM(6) and an entire company of soldiers could be transported in one LCM(8). The Navy modified LCM(6) ATC could only carry one platoon of 40 soldiers because of all the additional heavy armor that was added to the boat.[16] (USAMHI)

Chapter Two

MIKE BOATS

The Mekong Delta is a labyrinth of twisting rivers, waterways, and canals. The intricate manmade canal system was constructed during the nineteenth century to facilitate movement and open greater lines of communication for the Vietnamese population. These waterways were also considered to be better than any existing road network found throughout the entire country. The U.S. Army took advantage of this great mobility and deployed several medium boat companies to Vietnam beginning in 1965. These Army boat units operated landing craft to deliver combat troops and supplies to U.S. and allied forces fighting along the rivers and canals.[1]

A LCM(8) of the 1097th TC (MB) moves down the My Cong River in June 1968. Notice the large wake made by the ramp. "Outgoing tide on the rivers was about 10 knots, roughly the speed of most Army watercraft. An LCM could be running at full throttle against a tide and be stationary in the river."[2] (NARA)

Army medium boat units in Vietnam used 1950's vintage landing craft called the Landing Craft, Mechanized–Mark 8 [LCM(8)], which were nicknamed "Mike Boats." The LCM(8) was 73-feet long, twenty-four feet wide, and had a shallow draft that made the boat suitable for riverine combat. The hull was constructed of steel and was powered by two marine diesel engines and twin screws. The LCM(8) could carry a full infantry company or up to 260 short tons (STON) of cargo but they were very slow–capable of reaching only ten MPR when fully loaded. They were normally armed with two .50 Caliber M2 Machine Guns (MG), two 7.62-millimeter (mm) M-60 MGs, and one 40-mm M-79 Grenade Launcher (GL).

Landing Craft, Mechanized-LCM(8)

Purpose. . . . . To land a heavy tank or one of the larger vehicles during amphibious operations

Capacity. . . . . 120,000 lbs cargo

Crew. . . . . 5 men

Length overall. . . . . 73′ 7¾″

Beam. . . . . 21′ ⅛″ maximum

Draft. . . . . 5′ 2″ loaded

Full load displacement. . . . . 254,000 lbs

Hoisting weight. . . . . 134,000 lbs

Hoisted by. . . . . Sling

Construction. . . . . Semi-flat bottom, welded steel

Speed. . . . . 9 knots at full load displacement

Fuel capacity. . . . . 1,146 gallons

Range. . . . . 190 nautical miles at full power and full load

NavShips Drawing No. LCM(8) S0103-H-1387501

Stock No. . . . . SNSN S9-L-15153-1428

Engine details. . . . . 2 twin diesel units, 325 hp. each at 1,800 r.p.m. each utilizes two General Motors series
6-71 model 12005A, Model 12006A

Propeller details. . . . . 2—34″ D by 24″ P by 2½″ bore, 1 rh. and 1 lh. rotation

Cargo well. . . . . Approximate dimensions: 45′ 0″ long, 14′ 8″ wide, 4′ 3″ deep

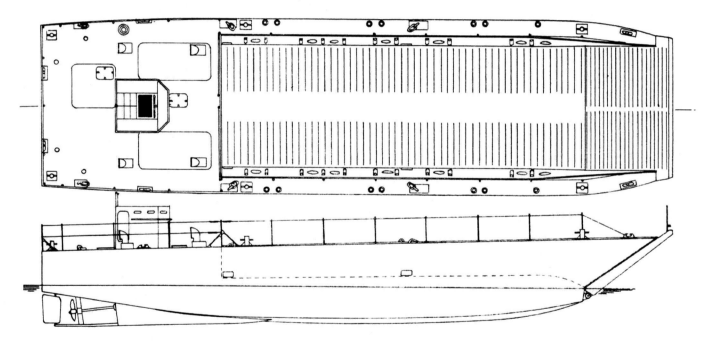

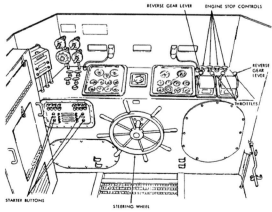

(above) The 73-foot LCM(8) specifications and general boat arrangements. The LCM(8) was originally designed to transport heavy tanks between ship and shore. Because of the increase size of modern tanks on the battlefield the Army replaced its smaller LCM(6) landing craft with the much more capable LCM (8).[3] (NAVSHIPS 250-452)

Drawing of the LCM(8) control station from an Army Technical Manual (TM). Army LCM crews normally consisted of six members; a coxswain, first mate, chief engineer, assistant engineer, and two seamen.[4] (U.S. Army)

An Army LCM(8) from the 1099th TC (MB) transports Army of the Republic of Vietnam (ARVN) soldiers along the Song Dong Tranh River during a riverine operation in August 1968. The 1099th also had two LCM(8)s that were modified into tactical offensive craft. "One had its welldeck covered with a platform so helicopters could land and the other had a 105mm howitzer and 4.2 inch mortars mounted on the deck."[5] (USAMHI)

An Army LCM(8) of the 1097th TC (MB) attached to the 9th ID is converted into an artillery FDC. The "Fly Swatter" shaped antenna was used with the AN/MRC VHF radio. The 1097th modified the well decks of other boats in the unit–one was converted into a first aid station, refueler, Prisoner of War (POW) interrogation center, and one boat even had a dayroom built for the crews' moral.[6] (USAMHI)

June 1968, LCM(8) Hull Number 66 moves along the My Cong River to conduct support operations for the 2nd Brigade (BDE), 9th ID. Notice the makeshift command center built in the well deck from wood and covered with mosquito netting. (NARA)

Three Army Medium Boat (MB) Companies were deployed to III CTZ from 1965–1968. The 1099th TC (MB) operated on the main rivers and canals providing direct support to the 199th LIB in the upper Mekong Delta. The 1099th TC (MB) also supported other infantry elements that operated in the swampy regions surrounding Saigon. The 544th TC (MB) deployed to "line haul" cargo on the rivers for combat units operating in the enemy infested Mekong Delta. The 231st TC (MB), United States Army Reserve (USAR), was activated following the 1968 TET offensive to transport vital supplies on the canals. The 1097th TC (MB) operated in IV CTZ and was attached to the 9th ID operating in the Mekong Delta.[7]

The LCMs would transport infantrymen ashore and remain on-station to provide emergency extractions or immediate fire support, if necessary. The versatile LCM(8) could carry large quantities of supplies and ammunition, which greatly reduced the combat load a soldier would normally have to carry on his back. They were also frequently used to push 65-foot barges and general cargo throughout the Delta. Some carried ten thousand-gallon bladders of JP-8 aviation gasoline (AVGAS) for helicopters, while others were used for

CPT Gary Wilde, Commanding Officer of the 1097th TC (MB), communicates with his other boats from the wheelhouse of an LCM(8) on the My Cong River, June 1968. The 1097th "River Raiders" became operational on 1 August 1967 and was the only tactical medium boat company in the Army's Transportation Corps.[8] (NARA)

An LCM(8) of the 1097th TC (MB) with a makeshift helicopter landing pad built on top of an AMMI pontoon, moves along the My Cong River, June 1968. The LCMs were not designed to tow barges, and took terrible beatings when conducting these types of operations.[9] (NARA)

Army marine engineers PFC Peter Meuse (left), and PFC Larry Puckett (right) work on a GM 6-71 Diesel Engine in the well deck of an LCM(8) in June 1968. LCMs were normally skippered by an enlisted sergeant.[10] The Army Military Occupational Specialty (MOS) for enlisted watercraft operators in Vietnam was 61 Bravo (61B). (NARA)

defoliation operations, spraying the vegetation along the rivers with toxic herbicides known as "Agent Orange." The LCM(8)'s cargo area was so spacious that they could be used to relocate entire villages, including livestock.[11]

Medium boat companies usually had seventeen LCM(8)s assigned; sixteen were task craft and one was a maintenance and salvage boat. The Army crews lived aboard their boats but the LCM(8)s did not have any factory installed living, latrine, or shower facilities onboard. This forced crews to use their imagination when performing basic chores like doing laundry–they placed bars of soap in their fatigue pockets and dragged the clothes behind the boat. The crews also built field expedient accommodations to make them more habitable during extended river operations. The "hootches" had to comply with certain height restrictions imposed by the Military Assistance Command Vietnam (MACV). In the Mekong Delta, boats could not be any taller than fifteen-feet so they could clear bridges at high tide during the wet season.[12]

Usually after about three weeks of combat, the boats would report back to their home base for scheduled maintenance and crew refit.[13] Despite the lack of speed–its cargo carrying capacity and semi-flat bottom hull made the LCM(8) an indispensible asset to riverine commanders in Vietnam.

An Army LCM(8) transports soldiers of the 9th ID on a canal in 1967. "The canals in Vietnam were just wide enough for an LCM to travel but noting larger. At the end of the canals there was a place wide enough to turn the boats around but otherwise the canals only allowed for one-way traffic."[14] (U.S. Army)

27 September 1966, two LCM(8)s are transporting cargo to shore form a supply ship anchored off the coast of South Vietnam at Vung Ro Bay. A Lighter, Amphibious, Resupply, Cargo-vehicle (5-ton) is parked in the foreground and piles of artillery ammunition are lying in the sand. Vung Ro Bay was a natural seaport that was unaffected by Vietnam's seasonal monsoons. (NARA)

An Army LCM(8) of the 1099th TC (MB) pulls a barge along the Song Van Co Tay River on 18 August 1967. Notice the sandbags piled up on the quarterdeck to protect the M2HB MG position and the canvas tarps attached to the wooden hootch on the stern. Canvas was added to the wooden structures after several boats were hit by enemy fire, which splintered the wood causing secondary injuries to the crew-members. (NARA)

LCM(8) of the 1097th TC (MB), 9th Supply and Transportation (S&T) Battalion (BN), is on a dry-dock barge for repairs at Naval Support Activity (NSA) Dong Tam in June 1968. Construction of wooden Command Posts (CP), Fire Direction Centers (FDC), and Mess Halls in the well decks and on the sterns were extremely sturdy, but over time insects and rodents became excessive. In areas where food was prepared they were particularly bothersome. Bugs and rats found their way onto the boats hiding inside of cardboard cartons and boxes.[15] (NARA)

A freshly painted Army LCM(8) in Vietnam. The large boat in the background is the *MV LTC John U. D. Page*, a container ship that was also operated by U.S. Army watercraft personnel. (Arlyn Musselman)

A U.S. Army "Mike Boat" with a modified control station built out of wood. This modification was purely for comfort and protection from the elements since the crews lived aboard the boats 24/7. The 544th TC (MB) built large hootches on the stern deck of their LCMs. The 1099th TC (MB) worked in conjunction with the 544th on the canals. The 1099th also built hootches but they were smaller and had collapsible masts so they could fit under the low bridges of III CTZ. After some time, the local population could identify the different units by the style of hootches built on the boats.[16] (James Burke)

An LCM(8) of the 544th TC (MB), which operated alongside the 1099th TC (MB) in the Mekong Delta. The 55 gallon drums on top of the makeshift wooden shack were filled with water and painted black so the sun could heat up the water, allowing the crews to take hot showers while on extended river operations. (Arlyn Musselman)

Members of Bravo Battery, 2nd BN, 4th Arty, 9th ID enjoy a stand down party in July 1969 after news that the unit is being withdrawn from Vietnam along with other elements of the 9th ID. Notice the soldier wearing boxer shorts and jungle boots. This was typically the uniform worn in Vietnam by crewman serving aboard LCM(8) landing craft because of the sweltering tropical climate. (NARA)

Chapter Three

MEKONG MONSTERS

In 1958, the Bell Aerosystems Company began producing a high-speed craft that could navigate effortlessly over both water and dry land on a cushion of air. The commercial development of hovercraft demonstrated superior performance over conventional amphibious vehicles and quickly caught the attention of the U.S. military. Bell first developed the Model 7232, Patrol Air Cushion Vehicle (PACV) for the U.S. Navy using a modified British SR-N5 hovercraft design. Three Navy PACVs were built and deployed to Vietnam in 1966 and evaluated under actual combat conditions. The results of the test were satisfactory, but improvements were necessary. So the PACVs were redeployed back to the United States to receive several upgrades.[1]

In 1966, the Army contracted Bell to develop its own version of the PACV. The U.S. Army Model 7255, SK-5, Air Cushion Vehicle (ACV) was designed to support infantry forces–it was wider, longer, and carried more weapons than the Navy PACV. It also carried 1,000 pounds of armor[2], had stronger side decks, and the front compartment door was widened to fit a Jeep inside of the cabin.[3] The ACV was powered by a gas turbine-turbo shaft, General Electric (GE) 7LM-100 PJ102 engine that produced 1,150-hp.[4] It had a 7-foot, 12-blade, centrifugal blower fan that forced air below the vehicle. Rubberized canvas skirts attached to the sides created a bubble, trapping the air, which lifted the vehicle off the surface. Forward motion was achieved by a variable pitch, Hamilton 3-blade aircraft propeller mounted on the rear deck. Both the lift-fan and propeller were powered by the same engine.[5]

SK-5 ACV Model 7255

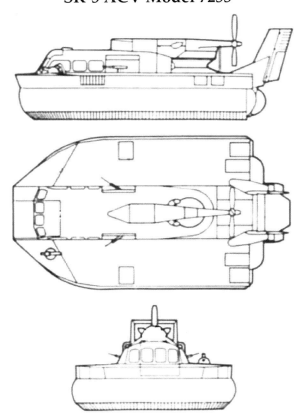

(Left) AACV 902 patrols along the My Tho River, 29 January 1969. The ACV was almost frictionless when it skimmed across the surface.[10] (NARA)

The manufacturing cost of an ACV was $1,000,000 so the Army only placed an initial order for three trial vehicles to determine if expanding the fleet was practical.[6] The first SK-5 Model 7255 ACV rolled off the production line in February 1968 and training was conducted at Aberdeen Proving Grounds, Maryland. The ACV platoon deployed to Vietnam in May 1968 with ACV hull numbers 901, 902, and 903. The unit was assigned to the 9th ID and operated from several different locations in the Mekong Delta. ACVs 901 and 902 had a vast array of offensive weapons installed and were designated as Assault Air Cushion Vehicles (AACV). ACV 903 was configured as a transport craft initially armed with only window mounted M-60 MGs and was designated as a Transport Air Cushion Vehicle (TACV).[7]

When riding on a cushion of air in open water, the ACV could reach speeds of nearly 70 MPR.[8] ACVs could easily maneuver through thick elephant grass, ditches, and canals. They could also clear small diameter trees and three-foot high vertical obstacles. They operated extremely well in rice paddies with low dikes and in wet–grassy areas such as the Plane of Reeds. Sometimes the weight of passengers limited the ACVs mobility, especially over hard ground.[9]

An artist rendition of an ACV concept vehicle. This painting is fairly accurate except for the dual XM75 Automatic Grenade Launchers (AGL) mounted on both sides of the cabin and the enclosed twin .50 Caliber MG turret positioned on top of the cabin. (USAMHI)

The ACVs provided riverine commanders the same mobility and shock effect that armored cavalry units had on dry land using APCs and air cavalry units using helicopters.[11] Ironically, the ACV had roughly about the same armor protection as APCs,[12] but they could carry more weapons and stay on station longer than helicopters. ACVs could carry up to twelve fully-equipped assault troops. During combat missions, the soldiers usually rode on the outside hull rather than sit inside of the hot, cramped cabin.[13]

Since there was no established doctrine, the ACV platoon used standard cavalry tactics and developed their own Standard Operating Procedures (SOP) from combat experience. They soon discovered that working in pairs was much better than operating alone, especially if one ACV got into trouble. Another preferred tactic when operating together was to have an experienced crewmember ride in a Light Observation Helicopter (LOH) to coordinate ACV movements from the air.[14] This provided ACVs advance warning of obstacles so they didn't have to slow down.[15]

Mechanical operation and maintenance were two major tasks confronted by the newly formed ACV platoon. For each operating hour, 2.1 hours of maintenance was required to keep the vehicles running. Combat damage caused most ACVs to be non-operational and mechanical failures were normally caused by the hydraulic and oil lubricating systems. Parts that were manufactured in

AACV-902 soon after it was delivered to the Army in February 1968 moves from land to water during crew training at Aberdeen Proving Grounds, Maryland. AACV-902 was the only vehicle that had a remote controlled XM75, 40-mm AGL mounted in an XM5 subsystem on the portside bow. The XM75 AGL had a range of 1,500 meters and could fire 230 rounds per minute.[16] (USAMHI)

AACV-902 races across the water at Aberdeen Proving Grounds, Maryland, in March 1968. The ACV was painted Federal Standard (FS) 34087 Olive Drab, which was also the same color of UH-1 Helicopters in Vietnam. The interior cabin was painted light gray.[17] (USAMHI)

TACV-903 conducts driver training at Long Binh, RVN, 17 May 1968. The driver could control vehicle movements at low speed by dumping air from four hydraulically activated skirt segments, or releasing cushion-air through four "puff ports" located on each side of the outer hull. The Puff Ports were added to the ACV to improve low-speed yaw control, and the Segmented Skirts increased the repair time of battle damage.[18] (NARA)

the United Kingdom had the tendency to fail prematurely. Obtaining repair parts was another problem–sufficient supplies were not available and had to be shipped directly from the United States.[19] In April 1969, only one spare engine was on hand. Organizational maintenance support was not established for the unit until late 1969. This caused AACV 901 to be unserviceable for nearly eight months because of a combat related accident in November 1968, which severely damaged the rear lift fan.[20] Repairs were not cost effective so the vehicle was scavenged for parts to keep the other two ACVs operational.[21]

Training was another unique challenge for the ACV unit. Because the platoon had only thirty-five soldiers authorized, no formal training course was established in the United States. Replacements learned how to operate and maintain the vehicles by unit personnel in Vietnam. A six-day driver course was established near Nha Be, which included extensive instruction on piloting the ACV over water. Upon completion, drivers were familiar enough with the ACVs unique operating characteristics, which gave them more confidence to negotiate more difficult terrain in combat.[22]

The ACV unit adopted the unofficial designation as the 39th Cavalry Platoon (ACV) and served in Vietnam until 31 August 1970.[23] Only one Army ACV survived the Vietnam War. AACV 901 was destroyed on 9 January 1970, and AACV 902 was destroyed on 4 August 1970, both by suspected land mines. TACV 903 was returned to the United States and is currently on display at the U.S. Army Transportation Museum at Fort Eustis, VA.

AACV-902 at Long Binh, RVN, 17 May 1968. An ACV could operate in combat for roughly five days without requiring any major mainte-nance. However, refueling in the field became a serious limiting factor for any prolonged operations.[24] (NARA)

An ACV returning to its base at Dong Tam upon completion of a mission in October 1968. Infantryman usually rode on the outer deck to enjoy the cool breeze. However, water spray during high speed operations would envelop the soldiers and turret gunners. Goggles or helicopter pilot helmets with built-in visors shielded the gunner's eyes so they could engage the enemy.[25] (NARA)

AACV 902 during Operation Truong Cong Dinh, 30 June–1 July 1968. The ACV Commander (CDR) rode in one of the turrets just like a tank commander but he was not completely visible to all of the crewmembers. He communicated with the accompanying infantry using hand and arm signals or with a squad radio. A flashing red beacon on top of the tail assembly was used to signal dismounted troops when it was time for extraction.[26] (NARA)

Interior view of an ACV control station in 1970. Internal communications was provided by a six-station intercom system. The factory installed AN/ARC-54 Frequency Modulated (FM) Radio System was unreliable in combat. At least one ACV was upgraded with a more dependable AN/VRC-46 Radio.[27] (NARA)

SP4 Donald Waltman, ACV gunner, 9th ID, mans his M-60D MG during a patrol in July 1968. The "D" model M-60 was designed for use as a helicopter door-gun. The range of the weapon was inadequate and it had no effect on bunkers. However, it did provide good suppressive fire for the infantry.[29] (NARA)

Staff Sergeant (SSG) Norman Reed, an ACV radar operator in July 1968. Excessive onboard noise was a misconception–ACVs were really just as loud as tracked vehicles. Crewmembers wore Combat Vehicle Crewman (CVC) or helicopter pilot helmets to communicate over intercoms.[31] (NARA)

Dong Tam, October 1968. Staff Sergeant James Waters cleans the mud off of his ACV with a pressure washer after completing a patrol. It was recommended to have seven soldiers assigned to each vehicle; a CDR, driver, radar navigator, senior gunner (turret), two side gunners, and an observer.[28] (NARA)

Dong Tam, October 1968. The crew of this ACV removes a damaged section of flexible skirt to install a replacement. The ACV had 12-piece skirts that consisted of outer trunks, a keel trunk, stability trunks, and rear bags. The skirts trapped a four-foot cushion of air, which made the ACV hover.[30] (NARA)

SSG Norman Reed demonstrates how to use the Decca 202 Radar Scope in July 1968. The radar was a valuable asset for day & night operations. It was critical that enlisted ACV navigators maintain proficiency on their equipment, so they could provide early detection of the enemy & obstacles.[32] (NARA)

An ACV at Dong Tam, preparing for Operation Truong Cong Dinh, 30 June–1 July 1968. The first ACV Platoon CDR was MAJ David G. Moore, who served from May 1968–April 1969. MAJ Moore was tasked to develop tactics and an SOP for the unit.[33] (NARA)

AACV-901 at Dong Tam being repaired after sustaining battle damage. Modern Hovercraft had a psychological effect on the indigenous Vietnamese population–they were enormous, noisy, fast, and earned the nickname "monster" from the enemy.[34] (Jim Bury)

A crane lifts AACV-902 for maintenance at Dong Tam in October 1968. ACVs weighed nearly eight-tons and could only be transported by CH-54 Skycrane helicopters. Since there were only three ACVs in Vietnam, a rotation schedule was established to keep at least one vehicle in maintenance while the other two were in the field. This helped the unit maintain operational readiness.[35] (NARA)

AACV-901 on stands for repairs at Dong Tam in July 1968. Sergeant (SGT) James Midkiff (right), and Corporal (CPL) Orval Kerr, inspects the hull to repair damaged sheet metal. On 2 July 1968, AACV-901 hit a high canal dike because the driver misjudged the slope. The accident caused the ACV to spin, which tore-off a twenty-foot section of the right skirt and dented a buoyancy tank.[36] (NARA)

An ACV picks up soldiers of 1st Platoon, Company C, 4th BN, 47th Infantry, 9th ID during a riverine operation in October 1968. Infantrymen riding on the deck risked falling into the lift-fan. This actually happened "during a November 1968 raid when an ARVN [sic] soldier, sitting near the lift fan intake, fell into the fan, resulting in his death. Attempts were made to correct this problem with a field expedient screen."[37] (NARA)

The XM-2 Mobile Personnel Detector (MPD) was sometimes mounted on ACVs to help pinpoint enemy locations. The MPD, more commonly referred to as the "people sniffer" was developed by GE to detect carbon and ammonia emissions commonly found in sweat and urine. While effective, people sniffers were sometimes oversensitive and would often detect body waste from animals, and could not differentiate between soldiers and civilians.[38] (NARA)

The dual gun turrets on top of the cabin provided a good field of vision, especially to the rear of the craft. The .50 Caliber gun mounts were fabricated locally by the unit. Armor protection for the turret gunners was inadequate so some crews welded large-steel ammunition cans to the ring mounts for extra protection.[39] (U.S. Army)

AACV-901 on riverine operations in 1970. The ACV carried heavy armor plates. The armor around the crew compartment could stop .30 Caliber rounds at 100 yards but it was removed to reduce vehicle weight. The plates that protected the engine, transmission, and fuel tanks could stop .50 Caliber rounds at 200 yards.[40] (USAMHI)

A VC prisoner is guarded on the deck of an ACV in 1970. Notice the screen on the rear deck. This was a field modification to prevent soldiers and equipment from falling into the lift-fan. (USAMHI)

An ACV maneuvers over a dry rice paddy in 1970. The ACV was a remarkable vehicle; it could maneuver over terrain that was impassible to tanks or wheeled vehicles. Although it was loud, the ACVs speed made up for the lack of surprise during attacks.[41] (USAMHI)

An ACV crosses a dry paddy field in 1970. Two M2 .50 Caliber MGs were originally installed in the turrets above the cargo compartment. ACV-903 had a third M2 mounted in the cargo bay, firing through the center window. Notice how the cabin window can open to the inside or out.[42] (USAMHI)

Aft view of an ACV moving over a field in 1970. The ACV had a 304-gallon self-sealing fuel tank but the vehicles could only operate for about seven hours before having to return to base for more fuel.[43] (USAMHI)

Front view of a Navy PACV at Dong Tam in 1967. Notice the differences when compared to the ACV like the sloping outer deck, small front hatch, and single turret on top of the cabin. The Navy PACV unit in Vietnam used the radio call sign "monster" and they painted large shark mouths on the front canvas skirts. (USAMHI)

An ACV during combat operations in 1970. The ACVs standard armament was changed in August 1970 by replacing one turret mounted M2 .50 Caliber MG with a GAU-2 minigun. The GAU-2 did provide good suppressive fire for the Infantry but the weapon system was unreliable–environmental effects caused malfunctions, it was difficult to aim, and it had excessive muzzle flash.[44] (USAMHI)

Front view of AACV-902 at Dong Tam in 1968. Notice the position of the Decca 202 Radar Scope and large space provided when the front hatch was fully opened. There was 65 square feet of interior cabin space and the outside flat decks were 6 feet wide on each side. The ACV also had approximately 6,000 lbs of emergency load lift capability.[45] (USAMHI)

Two ACVs on patrol in 1970. Notice their large silhouette. During their tour, no ACV ever received damage from sustained heavy caliber weapons. The only loss of an ACV was due to accidents and enemy mines. (USAMHI)

A team of ACVs are operating with two OH-6A LOHs to scout out the enemy in 1970. There were many similarities between ACV and helicopter operations. "In general, the ACVs became a kind of helicopter in permanent ground effect. Troop insertions and extractions took place in much the same manner and like helicopters."[46] (USAMHI)

TACV-903 on patrol with Army Rangers in the Plain of Reeds in 1970. Notice the bow-mounted .50 Caliber that was later replaced by a twin M60 MG rig. The Rangers are searching for hidden enemy weapon cashes using a mine detector.[47] (USAMHI)

Army Rangers of Echo Company, 75th Ranger Regiment, 9th ID "Go-Devil Rangers" patrol the Plain of Reeds on ACVs in 1970. The ACV was best suited for operations in swamps, paddies, and wetlands. The ACVs speed was affected when moving over hard surfaces. During Vietnam's dry season the water table was lower, which made paddy dikes higher and more difficult to climb.[48] (USAMHI)

An ACV patrols the Plain of Reeds in 1970 with 9th ID "Go-Devil Rangers." Providing overhead cover is a low flying OH-6A LOH. Helicopters sometimes had problems keeping up with ACVs when they operated at high speed in the Plain of Reeds.[49] (USAMHI)

An ACV patrols the Plain of Reeds in 1970 with 9th ID "Go-Devil Rangers." ACVs were ideal vehicles to insert or extract Long Range Reconnaissance Patrol (LRRP) Teams. Because of their loud noise, ACVs would deceive the enemy by making multiple "false" stops along the route to conceal the actual drop-off or pick-up locations.[50] (USAMHI)

A view of the ACVs GE 7LM100-PJ102 Engine. The ACV hull was divided into three parts, a center and two outer sections that could be broken down to facilitate shipment. The center section contained the engine, auxiliary power unit, fuel tank, tail unit, and the cargo compartment. The two outer hull sections were compartmentalized to provide buoyancy.[51] (NARA)

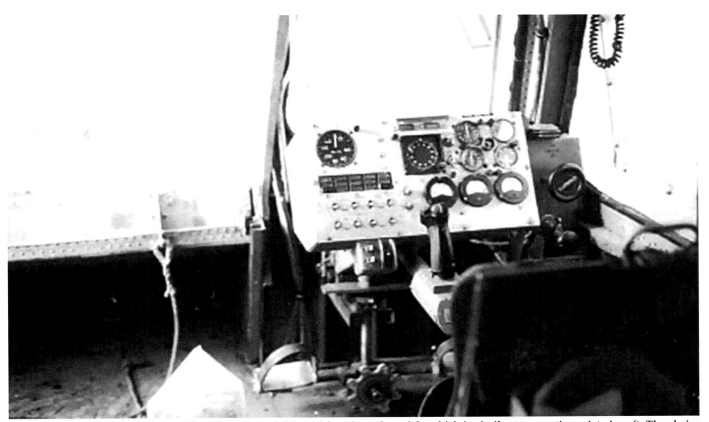

A view of an ACV control station. The driver steered the vehicle using a joy stick, which is similar to operating a jet aircraft. The chairs were armored and had seat belts similar to helicopters. (NARA)

SGT Mario Talon, XM5 gunner aboard AACV-902 makes final adjustments to his weapon system before a mission on 30 June 1968. The ACV carried 400 rounds of linked 40-mm ammunition for the XM75 AGL. The XM5 subsystem was originally developed for use on the UH-1 Iroquois Helicopter. The gunner operated the weapon using a remotely controlled electronic sight and trigger.[52] (NARA)

The crew of AACV-902 is preparing their vehicle for combat at Dong Tam on 30 June 1968. During an operation on 3 July 1968, a VC soldier was run over and killed by AACV-902. Also during this battle, the vehicles hydraulic system was damaged by enemy gunfire. The ACV broke contact to make temporary repairs and evacuate the wounded. Then it withdrew to a Special Forces (SF) camp at My Phouc Tay, where it made a hard nose-dive when parking.[53] (NARA)

SSG Cloyd Burton, ACV Commander, and SP5 Larry Casalengo, aircraft engine mechanic, reinstalls the auxiliary power unit aboard AACV-902 at Dong Tam on 30 June 1968. The ACV unit was equipped with an aircraft maintenance set "A" which was primarily used for UH-1 Helicopters. This photograph has a good view of the "puff-ports", which are the large square openings on the side of the ACV.[54]

Starboard aft view of TACV-903 on display at Fort Eustis, VA. The USARV desired to have a larger force of ACVs available for operations in Vietnam and, as a result, requested twelve ACVs; the Department of the Army later reduced this number to six. In the end, no further ACVs were produced, and none were sent to Vietnam because of astronomical acquisition costs.[55] (John Carrico)

An Army PBR cruising at high speed in blue water off the coast of Vietnam in 1970. The 458th TC (PBR) operated a small outpost at Vung Ro Bay, which was located south of Cam Ranh Bay. The port was operated by the 344th TC (Light Amphibian) and capable of handling two deep-draft vessels and stream discharge operations using barges, LCMs and LARC-Vs.[1] (Mike Hebert)

Unofficial pocket patch of the 458th TC (PBR).

Chapter Four

FANTASTIC PLASTICS

The U.S. Army was tasked to operate several inland and coastal ports in South Vietnam to facilitate the flow of ammunition and supplies delivered by merchant sea vessels. The U.S. Navy and Coast Guard were responsible for defending Vietnam's coastline and patrolling the inland waterways to interdict enemy supply lines. This security mission failed to adequately protect all of Vietnam's seaports, so the Army decided to organize its own harbor security force by assigning military policemen aboard Army watercraft.[2]

31' River Patrol Boat (PBR), MK 2

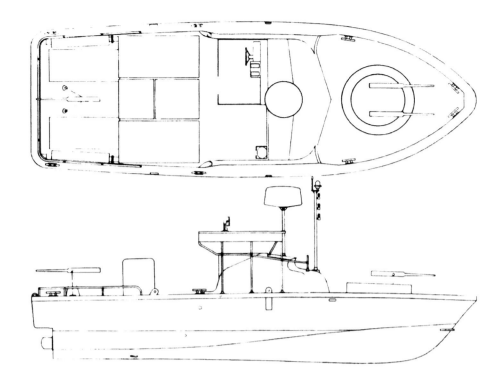

Purpose . . . . To patrol and secure the major rivers against infil-
tration by enemy craft

Capacity

Crew . . . . 4 men

Length overall . . . . 31'-11-1/2"

Beam . . . . 11'-7-1/2" maximum

Full load displacement . . . 16,000 lbs

Hoisting weight . . . . 16,000 lbs

Hoisted by. . . . . Slings

Construction . . . . V bottom fiberglass reinforced plastic

Speed

Fuel capacity. . . . . 160 gallons

Range

NavShips Drawing No.. . . . PBR31MK2-145-2490810

Stock No. 1940-926-1904

Engine details . . . . 2 Diesel propulsion engines, Detroit Diesel
6V53N, 216 HP @ 2,800 r.p.m.

Propeller details . . . . . . Two waterjet pumps

The 32-foot, fiberglass hulled PBR MK 2. Uniflite built thirty-nine PBRs specifically for the U.S. Army between 1967 and 1968. The large radar dome mounted on top of the cabin was designed to be lowered by removing a retaining pin and folding it down, so the boat could pass under low bridges. (NAVSHIPS 250-452)

The Army didn't have any specialized patrol boats in its inventory to perform waterborne security so it canvassed the other services for an adequate vessel. The Navy was using modified civilian boats to patrol on the rivers in Vietnam, so the Army decided to purchase the same boats to expedite the acquisition process. As an interim solution, the Army used various types of small boats called "Skimmers." Skimmer was a generic term given to outboard motorboats that ranged in size from 14-20 feet long. Skimmers were fast, maneuverable, easy to transport, and most had modified "V" bottom hulls.[3]

In 1967, the Army reorganized the 458th TC "Sea Tigers" into the Army's first Patrol Boat unit. The 458th TC (Light Amphibian) arrived in Vietnam on 13 October 1966 and was assigned the mission of transporting equipment from ship-to-shore using LARC-V amphibious vehicles. The 458th TC exchanged their LARCs for patrol boats and in August 1967, the unit received six Boston Whaler (BW) skimmers to begin harbor patrol duties. In April 1968, the 458th TC received its first ten PBRs at Vung Tau. The boats were delivered aboard the WWII Victory Ship, *SS Mercer Victory* and were prepared for combat in less than two weeks.[4] In all, the 458th TC operated thirty-nine PBRs, eighteen BWs, and had twenty-one outboard motors on hand. The unit was attached to the 18th Military Police (MP) BDE and re-designated as the 458th TC (Patrol Boat, River).[5] This was also the first time that an Army transportation company was assigned to a MP unit.[6] Military policemen assigned to the boats came from the 93rd, 95th, and 720th MP BNs.[7]

Four U.S. Army personnel were assigned to each PBR. Two Transportation Corps Soldiers served as the coxswain and engineer, two Army MPs served as gunners, and if available, a South Vietnamese marine policeman accompanied patrols to serve as an interpreter.[8] The Army PBR crews trained for four weeks at the Naval Inshore Operations Training Center (NIOTC) at Mare Island, California. Each of the soldiers were cross-trained in the operation of the boat, so if a crewmember was wounded or killed, anyone onboard could assume their duties and continue the mission.[9]

The 458th TC positioned detachments of PBRs and BWs at six Army ports, called "outports" in II and III CTZ. Three detachments were located at seaports along the coast of Vietnam in Qui Nhon, Vung Ro Bay, and Cat Lo. Three other detachments secured the inland waterway ports at Cat Lai, Newport/Saigon, and Nah Be. The HQ for the 458th TC was located at Di An, and a unit maintenance detachment was collocated with the Navy at Nha Be.[10] In total, the 458th TC patrolled 500 miles of inland waterways and canals. The PBRs and BWs searched sampans during the day, and set up ambushes at night to disrupt enemy movements. They conducted harbor and river patrols, and ammunition ship security missions.

Army port security operations continued up until 1 September 1971 when the 458th TC was inactivated and the boats turned over to the South Vietnamese.[11] The PBR and BW were truly "fantastic plastic" patrol craft, and a tremendous asset to the U.S. Army's harbor security force in Vietnam.

An Army PBR MK 2 on the Saigon River in 1970 just after completing a 180-degree turn and coming to a complete stop. The PBR could "dead-stop" from full speed in just thirty-two feet. This was accomplished because the water jet pumps had gates, which, when closed, redirected the outgoing streams of water in the opposite direction.[12] (NARA)

An Army LARC-V at Fort Lee, VA in June 1967. This is the type of amphibious vehicle that the 458th TC operated in Vietnam until the unit received patrol boats and transitioned to inland-water and port security duties that were previously performed by the U.S. Navy and Coast Guard.[13] (NARA)

Soldiers from B Company, 4th BN, 47th INF, 9th ID exit from a Boston Whaler in Long An province, 21 October 1967. The fiberglass BW was an extremely versatile craft that was used by many units in Vietnam. It was particularly useful for conducting waterborne ambushes where it could easily hide inside of the Nippa Palms that grew along the river banks. (NARA)

Soldiers from B Company, 4th BN, 47th INF, 9th ID patrol Long An province in Boston Whalers on 21 October 1967. The 9th ID had sixty BWs assigned in Vietnam. (NARA)

The Army's 458th TC had its own fleet of boats whose mission was to "provide, operate, and maintain patrol craft for the security of ports within the RVN by interdicting enemy supply lines, by conducting close-in port surveillance, and by detecting and destroying enemy waterborne offensive capabilities."[14] (U.S. Army)

An Army PBR MK 2 comes to an abrupt stop during a demonstration run. Inexperienced crewmembers might find themselves overboard if they weren't holding on to something attached to the vessel. Boats with outboard engines were not capable of stopping in such a short distance. (U.S. Army)

An MP assigned to the 18th MP BDE mans the forward gun position on an Army PBR MK 2. Twin MGs were used on PBRs to increase the chances of hitting a target from a fast moving boat. Notice the flash suppressors attached to the end of the .50 Caliber MG barrels. The forward "fifties" were fired by a single trigger that was connected to electronic solenoids attached to the butt-plate. (U.S. Army)

A 458th TC PBR MK 2, hull number J-7836 in 1969. The 450-watt searchlight for the forward gun tub was installed in a specially designed "shock mount" by attaching springs to suspend the light inside of an eight-quart household cooking pot. So theoretically when the .50 Caliber MGs fired, the searchlight would remain steady and not shake violently with the recoil. (NARA)

An Army PBR MK 2 from the 458th TC patrols a river near Saigon in May 1971. The PBR only needed two-feet of water to operate and could literally skim over the surface at high speeds as evident in the photo. The sign on the side of the coxswain flat identifies the boat as a MP vessel. (NARA)

A color shot of PBR MK 2 J-7836. The unique camouflage pattern was applied to the boat by its crew. All PBRs manufactured by Uniflite were painted Marine Corps Green Shade #23 (FS34052). The camouflage pattern used here was a light olive green color. PBR J-7836 was the only boat stationed at Qui Nhon that was painted camouflage.[15] (Jerry Wallace)

A damaged PBR MK 2 of the 458th TC at Cat Lai in May 1971. The PBR was an extremely rugged craft and could take a beating. The speed of the boat provided some degree of protection from VC gunners who were typically bad shots. Since the boat was made of fiber-glass, sometimes RPG rounds would go completely through the boat without detonating. Notice how the boats are parked with the stern facing the dock. This was done so the crews could board and maneuver the boats quickly away from the docks. (NARA)

PBRs J-7813 (closest to the dock), J-7814, and J-7815 at Vung Tau in December 1969. Notice the retractable light masts–the mast on PBR J-7814 is lowered and the light mast on PBR J-7813 is fully raised. The soldier standing on the bow is SP4 Robert Brower who was stationed at the Cat Lo outport and served as boat captain on PBR J-7813. Bob is helping to restore the only surviving Army PBR from the Vietnam War–PBR J-7844 was one of three Army PBRs built in 1970 as a replacement for damaged boats in Vietnam. The boat was never shipped because of the 1969 Vietnamization Program and was instead sent to Fort Eustis, VA, for harbor security duty. The boat was sold several years ago at a government sale to a private collector, and is now at Bellingham, WA, for full restoration.[16] (Robert Brower)

River Patrol Boat MK 2

The Patrol Boat, River (PBR) was originally developed in 1965 because of an urgent request by the U.S. Navy to find a suitable patrol boat that could operate in the shallow-waters of South Vietnam. The contract was won by Uniflite (United Boatbuilders) of Bellingham, Washington, who developed the 31-foot PBR MK 1 by using a commercial off-the-shelf fiberglass cabin cruiser hull and a Navy-designed superstructure.[17] The 32-foot PBR MK 2 was developed in 1967 and incorporated several improvements over the earlier MK 1. Thirty-nine PBR MK 2s were built by Uniflite for the U.S. Army under the Expedited Non-Standard Urgent Requirement for Equipment (ENSURE) Program 157[18] for $86,000[19] each, which did not include the cost of weapons and additional military hardware.

The PBR MK 2 could operate in water as shallow as two feet, and could cruise up to 37 MPR under the power of its two 6V53N Detroit Diesel marine engines and twin 14YJ Jacuzzi Brothers water-jet drives.[20] Jet pumps were used instead of propellers because they provided greater maneuverability in the weed-choked waterways of Vietnam.[21] The PBR was also a very stable craft, which was particularly useful in port areas because water usually turned choppy during the hours of darkness. Although PBRs could operate in extremely shallow water, tidal depths sometimes limited patrol areas–during low tides PBRs would have to remain in the harbors or deep river channels to avoid being damaged by sandbars.[22]

The PBRs standard armament included a Mark-56 Mod-0 universal gun turret installed on the bow that mounted two M2 .50 Caliber MGs; a Mark-46 Mod-1 tripod mount was installed on the stern that held a single M2 .50 Caliber MG; an M-60 7.62-mm MG and Honeywell Mark-18 40-mm GL was mounted amidships above the engines.[23] Individual weapons included two M-79 40-mm GLs, three M-16 rifles, one 12-gauge shotgun, and one .38 Caliber pistol. The MPs assigned to the boats preferred using shotguns when inspecting sampans because they were easy to use and had a wide shot pattern when fired.[24] The PBRs onboard firepower was adequate for the mission. However, many soldiers would have preferred replacing all of the M2s with M-60 MGs because strict permission was required from higher authority before firing any large caliber weapons around populated areas.[25]

Protection for the crewmembers was provided by ballistic plates installed on the gun mounts, on top of the engine covers, and surrounding the coxswain station. These plates were designed to withstand a direct hit from .30 Caliber ball ammunition. Crews were satisfied with the location and characteristics of the ballistic plates and additional protection was provided by wearing body armor and steel helmets.[26]

The PBR was equipped with a Raytheon 1900N/D limited-range, high-resolution, low-error, Plan Position Indicator (PPI) Radar System.[27] The radar was mainly used for night patrols, but interviews with Army PBR crews in 1970 revealed that the system was rarely used because of non-operational equipment and a lack of proper training.[28]

For communications, the PBR had an AN/VRC-49 limited-range FM radio system that operated with in the Very High Frequency (VHF) band and was also equipped with retransmission capability. The AN/VRC-49 System was essentially two AN/VRC-46 transceivers that operated independently and had separate antennas, a remote control box, and auxiliary loudspeakers. Both transceivers were enclosed in watertight cases and mounted on a shock-insulated platform located inside of the cabin.[29] The dual Radio System was used to monitor separate command and operational networks–the MP operational frequency was used to dispatch and control the boats.[30] The AN/VRC-46 transceivers had a high deadline rate, so quite often only one radio was operational, which severely limited PBR communications during patrols.[31]

The PBR was an agile craft that was suitable for harbor security missions. However, some operational and safety concerns were observed. A major problem was discovered with the PBRs electrical system, which caused the total loss of one boat because of an electrical fire. The 458th TC did not have trained electricians, so boat crews usually applied field expedient wiring corrections that compounded the problem.[32] The harsh operating conditions in Vietnam also wreaked havoc on boat components, causing them to fail prematurely–heat; humidity, oxidation, sea life, and floating debris caused most of the damage. Saltwater caused excessive corrosion and silt abrasion damaged the stainless steel Jacuzzi pumps, so some parts were replaced by magnesium/bronze alloy that was less susceptible to environmental effects and lasted much longer.[33] Water debris also damaged the electric bilge pumps, so many crews scavenged parts from deadlined boats, or replaced the original pumps altogether with similar ones taken off APCs because sufficient quantities of PBR repair parts were not readily available.[34]

Operational readiness was another challenge that affected PBR operations. On average, thirteen PBRs per day were deadlined for maintenance issues which left only twenty-six boats to meet daily mission requirements. This caused a severe strain on the operational boats forcing some to patrol twenty-four hours a day. In some instances, BWs had to be substituted for PBRs, and at one outpost a PBR actually operated for 79 consecutive days without going in for any required maintenance.[35] Engines were usually damaged from overheating, oil or fuel contamination, and poor lubrication.[36] The PBR engines needed to be warmed-up before operations and cooled-off before shutting them down. If these procedures were not followed, the engine cylinder sleeves and heads could crack.[37]

Repair parts were not stocked at any Army Depot in Vietnam or in the United States, so MACV established a separate technical supply account at Cam Ranh Bay. While the Army Supply System was being organized, an inter-service support agreement was reached between the 458th TC Maintenance Detachment at Nha Be, and the U.S. Navy. The agreement allowed the Army to purchase up to $15,000 worth of boat parts per month. The Navy also provided emergency repair parts if they had sufficient qualities on hand. Ultimately, the Army acquired about ten-percent of its repair parts from the Navy.[38] "Another source of PBR parts was cannibalization of equipment turned in for repair. Four PBRs were cannibalized to the extent that they had to be turned in for depot-level refitting in October 1969."[39]

Despite some deficiencies, Army PBRs performed harbor security duties exceptionally well. The crews were satisfied with the PBRs high-speed mobility and capacity to operate in shallow water, on inland waterways, and within port areas. The onboard weapons provided a high volume of suppressive fire and the fiberglass hull required minimum care and were not easily damaged by waterborne hazards.[40]

An Army PBR MK 2 on the Saigon River in 1970 makes a 180-degree turn at high speed. Intricate maneuvers like this were easily accomplished if the boat was driven by an experienced coxswain. Barely visible above the engine spray is the white hull number J-7830. The "J" hulls were specifically built by Uniflite for the Army, and Navy PBR hull numbers began with "31RP." Unless there were visible MP markings on the side of the boat, the hull number was the only way to tell the difference between Army and Navy PBRs. (NARA)

PBR MK 2 J-7841 is literally skimming across the water during a high-speed maneuver near Cat Lai in 1970. Notice the large shiny object in the rear of the boat near the .50 Caliber MG mount. These were stainless steel mufflers that were normally hidden by insulated plastic covers installed on both sides of the boat. Also notice the paint scuffs and chips on the aluminum gunwales. The earlier PBR MK 1s did not have any protection along the sides of the boat and were easily damaged when inspecting Vietnamese sampans. (Jerry McDevitt)

"Death Dealers" was a PBR MK 2 assigned to 458th TC Vung Ro Bay outport. Notice the bright blue water that Army PBRs operated in off the coast of South Vietnam. Most people associate PBR operations with the muddy brown water of the Mekong Delta. (Mike Hebert)

A starboard bow view of Army PBR MK 2 J-7832 just after a patrol in 1970. Notice the portable AM/FM Radio on top of the cabin and the M-69 Flak Vests attached to the hand-rails. A technique frequently used at night in Vung Ro Bay was to shut off the PBRs engines and drift silently, listening for sounds and looking toward lighted areas for movement. The crews occasionally allowed themselves to be decoys to draw enemy fire.[41] (Mike Hebert)

An Army PBR at Vung Ro Bay in 1970. For many soldiers, the small harbor looked like paradise with its single pier jutting into the crystal blue water. On the other side of the ridge in this photograph it looked like a moonscape. Trees had been blasted and defoliated—it was eerie looking and a Korean Infantry unit was stationed nearby to keep guerrilla activity in check.[42] (Mike Hebert)

The "Magic Christian" was the nickname given to Army PBR J-7832. Mike Hebert from Laurel, Maryland, was the boat coxswain and is pictured here refueling his boat in 1970. The PBR MK 2 had two-eighty gallon fuel tanks that powered the diesel engines. (Mike Hebert)

An almost tranquil scene of an Army PBR MK 2 making a hard starboard turn at Vung Ro Bay, South Vietnam, in 1970. The PBR had two dry-chemical fire extinguishers onboard to fight fires. Crewmembers considered these inadequate. The loss of a boat at Cat Lo in May 1969 demonstrated that dry-chemical extinguishers were not sufficient to put out electrical fires. It was suggested that two CO_2 fire extinguishers be carried on the boats to eliminate this problem.[43] (Mike Hebert)

On 28 June 1970, Army PBR MK 2 J-7832, the "Magic Christian" was hit by an enemy B-40 RPG on the East side of Vung Ro Bay. Amazingly, all of the crewmembers survived the attack. The armor plate that protected the forward gunner was ripped in half like it was a piece of paper. (Mike Hebert)

Two maintenance soldiers work on the engines of a PBR at Cat Lai in 1969. The PBR had two marine 6V53N water-cooled engines that were manufactured by Detroit Diesel (formally GM Diesel). Each engine produced 216-hp and were connected directly to the Jacuzzi jet-pumps by flexible drive shafts. The 6V53N engine had six, two-stroke valves set up in a "V" configuration that displaced 53 cubic inches per cylinder, and were naturally aspirated using atmospheric pressure to draw in combustion air.[44] (Thomas Wonsiewicz)

Soldiers water skiing behind an Army PBR MK 2 near Vung Ro Bay in 1970. Considered by many to be an urban legend, soldiers and sailors actually water skied in Vietnam much like the famous scene in the Hollywood film, *Apocalypse Now*. (Mike Hebert)

Two hard working soldiers on a PBR that is undergoing repairs in 1969. The diesel engines used a high compression-ignition system as opposed to gasoline engines that use sparkplugs. They also had a high thermal capacity allowing them to operate for extended periods under heavy payloads. However, diesel machinery is heavier than gasoline engines and they produced a lot more vibration and noise. Therefore, PBR engines were mounted on top of rubber mounts to eliminate vibrations and the engine compartments were insulated to reduce excessive noise. [45] (Thomas Wonsiewicz)

Two Army PBRs and a Boston Whaler docked at the Cat Lai outport in 1969. The boats used standard marine bumpers or small aircraft tires to protect the sides and stern of the boat. Just visible above the waterline are the jet-pump deflectors. (Thomas Wonsiewicz)

A view of a complete Jacuzzi Brothers 14YJ jet-pump still in the shipping crate. The water-jet drive system was considered adequate but excessive wear caused decreased efficiency of the pumps. This was caused mainly by debris and silt found in the RVN waterways and was compounded by the lack of replacement parts.[46] (John Carrico)

The retractable light mast mounted on PBRs had three colored globe lights made by Perko that were welded to the front, and above each other. Positioned on top of the mast was a WWII vintage Nancy Beacon that had a dark blue lens. Inside of the lens was a light bulb, which was shielded by a thin metal sleeve that had a small opening on the top. The opening emitted just enough light to be detected from the air so PBRs could send distress signals to helicopters in morse code.[47] (NARA)

The Honeywell Mark-18 40-mm GL was mounted on the starboard-aft ballistic plate of Army PBRs. The Mark-18 was operated by a hand-crank which fed the linked 40-mm ammunition through the breach.[48] The Mark-18 was an ideal weapon for suppressive fire and could cover an area the size of a football field with twenty-four deadly grenades in ten seconds.[49] However, the Mark-18 had a high misfire rate because of faulty ammunition belts, firing pins, and rough cycling action when trying to achieve a higher rate of fire. Many Army PBR crews used an additional M-60 MGs in lieu of the Mark-18 GL because of high Not Operationally Ready (NOR) rates and lack of repair parts.[50] (NARA)

A female South Vietnamese Interpreter enjoys an American soft drink onboard PBR J-7836. She is wearing a snug fitting Vietnamese tiger striped uniform, which was also manufactured in western sizes. Tiger Striped fatigues were prized possession among PBR crews. Notice the Sireno ED-1 model siren mounted on the deckhouse. The siren was used in conjunction with the boats bull horn to signal suspicious watercraft to stop. A verbal command "HALT" was issued once in English and three times in Vietnamese over the bull horn. If the command was not followed, the PBRs siren was used to draw attention. If the siren was ignored, and the suspicious craft took evasive maneuvers, it could be overtaken and fired upon.[51] (Angelo Rossetti)

One outport detachment obtained a U.S. Navy 60-mm mortar and installed in the aft gun position of an Army PBR. The naval 60-mm mortar could be used for direct-fire by pulling a trigger or indirect-fire by dropping a round into the tube like a conventional mortar.[52] (U.S. Army)

Boston Whaler

In 1967, the Army acquired several flat-bottom skiffs called Boston Whalers for use in Vietnam. The Boston Whaler was also called a Motor Boat Plastic (MBP), "Skimmer" or simply a "BW". The BW was primarily used for patrolling, harbor security, transport, and oil spill recovery operations. Because of its small size and shallow draft, they could search locations that larger PBRs could not reach, like under piers, close-in inspection of ship hulls, or in extremely shallow waterways. The BW was also used to drop concussion grenades in the water near ships to deter enemy Sappers from emplacing explosive charges.[53] Other commercial skimmers were used in Vietnam like the Miami Surfer[54] and a larger version of the BW that was several feet longer, a little wider in the beam, had an additional bench seat, no steering console, and was primarily used as a transport vessel.[55]

Army BWs were obtained under ENSURE 33.1[56] and were commercially built by Fisher & Pierce Manufacturing in Rockford, Massachusetts.[57] The BW was 16-foot, 7-inches long, made of fiberglass, and cost $3,500 each to produce. The BW normally carried a crew of two–three soldiers and was powered by either an 80/85-hp, or a 40-hp Johnson outboard motor. It had a maximum payload of 2,400 pounds, and could carry either ten passengers with light equipment or seven fully combat-equipped passengers. The BW could attain speeds of 35 to 40 MPR, depending upon the motor used, and it drew twenty-two inches of water with the motor lowered. The BW had no organic armament or communication equipment, relying solely upon crew-carried weapons and radios.[58] Some BW assigned to the 458th TC mounted an M-60 MG on a pedestal mount, similar to the ones used on gun-Jeeps.[59] The BW had a double laminated "W" (trimaran) fiberglass hull with block foam flotation, which made it virtually unsinkable.[60]

The BW was durable and satisfactory for its assigned patrolling missions. Nevertheless, the boats large coxswain station reduced its usefulness for hauling cargo or litter patients so a design change was recommended to reduce the size of the control console.[61] Additionally, the BW didn't handle very well in rough water and some crews suggested that the rim around the top of the boat be reinforced to make it more sturdy.[62] Some BW crews also disliked the Johnson 40-hp motors because they did not provide sufficient power for high-speed patrolling.[63] Running strait motor gasoline (MOGAS) was found to cause engine problems but by mixing one-part JP-8 AVGAS with two-parts MOGAS this produced an acceptable fuel for the BW.[64]

Maintenance issues caused high NOR rates for BWs. For instance, there were eighteen BWs assigned to the 458th TC and on average only eleven were operational each month primarily because of engine problems.[65] "The 458th TC was not authorized to perform extensive repair on outboard motors. However, the unit had become self-supporting and performed all maintenance and repairs, including complete overhauls, when parts were available."[66]

The BW was an excellent choice to complement the PBR for harbor security duties. It was more reliable and outperformed other small watercraft in its class. The military also conducted several experiments on BWs in Vietnam. A hydrofoil equipped BW was built and tested but deemed unsatisfactory for routine patrol work. There was also one BW "Quiet Fast Boat" that was powered by an experimental quiet outboard motor.[67]

An Army BW of the 458th TC sits on the beach at Vung Ro Bay, South Vietnam in 1970. BWs proved to be satisfactory for harbor security operations. However, some outports were forced to improvise a control console as evident here.[68] (Mike Hebert)

Boston Whaler

Length - 16 feet 7 inches

Beam - 70 inches

Draft - 18 inches

Max Capacity - 2,400 lbs

Weight - 730 lbs

Material - Fiberglass

Transom Height - 20 inches

Cost - $3,500

A 458th TC BW at Vung Ro Bay in 1970. This BW just received a fresh coat of O.D. paint. Notice the color contrast between the BW and PBR sitting in the background, which was painted Marine Corps Green #23. The soldiers painting the boat used their personal flair and added a red stripe at the waterline and around the engine cover. (Mike Hebert)

An Army BW from the 2nd Platoon, B Company, 720th MP BN operates at high-speed to intercept a Vietnamese Sampan on the Song Dong Nai River in April 1968. Notice the antenna and radio headset worn by the coxswain. The BW did not have any organic communications equipment installed so this crew used a portable AN/PRC-25 radio to coordinate patrol activities. (NARA)

An Army BW from the 2nd Platoon, B Company, 720th MP BN patrols the Song Dong Nai River in April 1968. This boat has an M-60 MG mounted on the bow. Although MGs were not necessarily accurate when fired from a moving boat, they did provide a good degree of suppressive fire. (NARA)

An Army BW from the 458th TC patrols the Saigon River on 27 February 1970. The gunner is SP4 Rossi, an Army MP, and the Coxswain is "Red" Roemer, an Army Transportation Corps Soldier. This boat is powered by a Johnson 80/85-hp outboard motor. (NARA)

Soldiers from 1st Platoon, A Company, 1st BN, 27th INF, 25th ID, unloads a BW from a 5-ton truck in March 1968. The BW was relatively lightweight and easy to transport. Notice the hand rails that were not always installed on some BWs. (NARA)

Soldiers from the 25th ID use ores to push a BW into deeper water so they can start the outboard motor during an operation in March 1968. The soldiers are wearing B-7 Life Preservers. The B-7 was worn under the arms and was operated by pulling strings attached to CO_2 cartridges, which inflated two large yellow balloons that kept the soldier afloat if falling overboard. (NARA)

When the BWs arrived in country, they were equipped with both 40 and 80-hp motors. Johnson stopped making the 80-hp model engine during the war and began producing an 85-hp outboard, which became their standard motor. Crews soon discovered that many of the parts between the two models were not interchangeable, causing some BWs to become NOR due to the lack of correct repair parts.[69] (Mike Hebert)

(below) An Army BW conducts a physiological operation (PSYOPS), loud-speaker mission near Da Nang in March 1969. The Vietnamese soldier speaking into the handset is Nhan Ngoc Mai, a Kit Carson Scout who was formally an enemy soldier but surrendered under the Chieu Hoi Program.[70] Kit Carson Scouts were invaluable for conducting tactical interrogations of enemy prisoners and were particularly effective for PSYOPS missions that required Vietnamese language skills.[71] (NARA)

Two BWs tied-up to a dock at an Army outport. Notice the two red portable fuel tanks in each boat and the Johnson 80/85-hp outboard motors. The BW was required to operate at fast and slow speeds–slow speeds were needed to patrol the congested waterways. Many crews discovered that operating the engines at slower speeds caused a high rate of carbon buildup and battery drainage. To alleviate this problem, a smaller 9.5-hp motor was issued to some units to be used in conjunction with the 80/85-hp motor.[72] (James Burke)

PFC Oscar McKnight, Radio Operator from B Company, 39th INF, 9th ID prepares to jump from a BW after patrolling the Song Nha Be River on 11 December 1967. These particular boats do not have steering consoles and are manually navigated by a throttle-bar attached directly to the 40-hp Johnson motor. Observe that the plastic covers have been removed from the motors to prevent overheating. (NARA)

Chapter Five

AIRBOATS

During the spring of 1964, the U.S. Army Special Forces (SF) in Vietnam submitted a request to the Commander, United States Military Assistance Command Vietnam (COMUSMACV) for a fast, shallow-draft boat that could carry up to five fully-equipped combat troops and was capable of operating in swampy terrain. At the time no such watercraft existed in the military supply inventory, so the Army looked to the Navy for suggestions. In 1961, the U.S. Navy had tested several civilian airboats in Vietnam, which were similar to the ones being used in the Florida Everglades for hunting and pleasure tours. The Army quickly purchased twelve airboats for a new assessment.[1]

A Hurricane airboat on display at the War Memorial of Korea located in Seoul, South Korea. This is possibly the only wartime Aircat on display. Airboats were particularly useful to patrol a vast swamp southeast of Saigon called the Rung Sat Special Zone (RSSZ). Rung Sat means "Forest of Assassins" in Vietnamese. Here the VC operated with impunity in a swamp that had thousands of twisting waterways that looked like a giant maze from above.[2] Installed directly behind the Airboat driver's seat was a metal protective cage that surrounded the engine and propeller blade. This was necessary to keep occupants and foreign objects away from the dangerous propeller. (MAJ Mandy MacWhirter)

Two types of commercial airboats were sent to Vietnam for evaluation–the Susquehanna Skimmer and the Hurricane Aircat. The Skimmer was manufactured at the Danville Airport in Danville, Pennsylvania. The Hurricane Fiberglass Products Company in Auburndale, Florida, manufactured the Aircat. The government asked each company to build six prototypes for the evaluation and paid approximately $6,000 per boat.[3] Both airboats were seventeen feet long and roughly seven feet wide; they weighed 1,200 pounds empty and had twin rudder steering. They both also had the same 88-hp Lycoming 0-360 air-cooled gasoline engine installed. The Skimmer had a semi "V" bottom hull constructed of fiberglass and 3/8-inch plywood, and the Aircat had a semi-catamaran hull made entirely of molded fiberglass.[4]

The Aircat and Skimmer were built by small private companies, which had limited manufacturing capabilities. This caused several delays in production, and the boats did not arrive in Vietnam until October 1964. An airboat-training program was established immediately after the Airboats arrival, but they were not employed in the field until 7 November 1964. By then, water levels had receded in Vietnam causing Phase I of the evaluation to be terminated. Because insufficient data was collected to draw final conclusions and recommendations, a Phase II evaluation was conducted during the 1965 rainy season by Vietnamese Special Forces operating in the Plain of Reeds.[5]

The testing revealed exactly what the Navy had learned three years earlier; high engine and propeller noise reduced the element of surprise. However, it was soon discovered that when two or more boats operated in the same area, it was nearly impossible to determine the exact number or the direction the Airboats were traveling unless the enemy could actually see them. This was usually impossible because of restricted visibility in swamps and marshlands, and the low silhouette and high speed of the Airboats. This also caused an adverse psychological effect on the enemy. In order to achieve surprise, the noise made by other airboats or helicopters was used to deceive the enemy. It was possible to maneuver airboats practically undetected under this umbrella of noise. Two to three airboats maneuvering together was a much better tactic than deploying one airboat alone.[6]

Problems were soon discovered with the Susquehanna Skimmers. The exhaust system was poorly designed and made of low quality material, which caused many systems to fail because of engine vibrations. A modified stainless steel exhaust manifold was built for the Skimmers and installed late in the evaluation that were much more reliable.[7] There were also problems with the Skimmers hull, which deteriorated very rapidly and caused a high demand for maintenance. In addition, the tropical climate in Southeast Asia had an adverse effect on the machinery and instruments, which accelerated the wear and tear of many components. The Skimmers out-

An experimental JBX-21 airboat undergoes stateside testing by the U.S. Army in the early 1960s. The JBX-21 had a 20-foot aluminum hull, four-blade propeller, and was powered by a 400-hp aircraft engine. The Airboat was designed to transport a squad of soldiers over marshy terrain and it had a top speed of 35 MPR. However, the massive 400-hp engine produced excessive noise, so ultimately the JBX-21 was not accepted by the Army.[8] (U.S. Army)

Not an exceptionally good photograph from an Army TM, but the only one I could find of a Susquehanna Skimmer Airboat in Vietnam. Mr. Kenneth Burrows, who designed the Airboat, was a pioneer in the Aviation Industry. He was an instructor pilot when WWII started at a training field near Harrisburg, PA. After the war, he opened his own airport in Danville, PA where he flew several single engine planes and taught hundreds of students how to fly. He also owned an auto repair shop that was connected to the airport and this is where he built six Susquehanna Skimmers in 1964 that were evaluated by the U.S. Army.[9] (U.S. Army)

A Hurricane Aircat airboat from the 5th SF Group (ABN) makes a high speed firing run with its .30 Caliber, A-6 MG. The pintle mount was installed six inches from the rear of the bow decking to allow gunners to traverse 180 degrees. This airboat has been nicknamed "Jo Ann," which is painted in white letters on the bow. The first airboat was invented by Dr. Alexander Graham Bell with the help of his engineers; he called it the "Ugly Duckling."[10] (U.S. Army)

One of sixty airboats assigned to Detachment A-404, 5th SF Group (ABN). This airboat is patrolling in Kien Phong Province, South Vietnam on 28 August 1969. Airboats were exceptionally fast—so crews learned very quickly to keep their mouths closed when operating at high speeds in swamps or they would be eating grasshoppers and other indigenous bugs.[11] (NARA)

preformed the Aircats in deep water. However, the Skimmer could not easily navigate rice paddies. The Aircat could effortlessly jump across paddy dikes that were at least two feet tall and at speeds of twenty MPR without apparent damage to the hull. The Skimmers sustained considerable hull damage when operating cross-country.[12]

On 2 November 1965, one Skimmer struck a five-foot high obstacle at high-speed. The hull was severely damaged and three soldiers were injured. For tactical reasons, the ruined hull was destroyed in place with demolitions.[13] At the end of Phase II testing, two Skimmers were non-operational with thrown piston rods. The remaining three were running, but required general overhauls. All of the hulls deteriorated so badly that they also required major repairs. The plywood base of the Skimmers hull did not withstand the tropical environment and were found to be unsatisfactory for Vietnam.[14]

Of the original six Aircats, one was lost in an accident and the remaining five were still operational at the end of the evaluation period with all of them requiring general overhauls. Engines needed complete replacement of seals, spark plugs, and magnito points. Four boat frames required repair for cracks located near the engine mounts and the oil coolers on two boats required servicing to free stuck thermostat valves.[15] No repair or maintenance capability had been established during the testing period, so U.S. aviation mechanics were used to perform repairs. Because the Airboats used aircraft engines, "even the most elementary engine repair work required the attention of a skilled mechanic or factory-trained specialist."[16]

A 5th SF Group (ABN) Aircat airboat jumps over a rice paddy dike in the Mekong Delta in 1966. Advanced and individual airboat training was conducted at Moc Hoa and Cai Cai, South Vietnam. Airboats were capable of jumping over rice paddy dikes by executing several 180 degree turns to spray it down with water then going straight over. If an airboat hit a dry paddy dike it would stop instantly and anyone not wearing a seatbelt would be ejected from the boat and severely injured or killed.[17] (U.S. Army)

The Hurricane Aircat was selected for use by the Army but several modifications were necessary to meet military standards and operational requirements in the RVN. An initial production request of 54 airboats was sent to the manufacture along with a summary of required changes.[18] Some critical deficiencies that were identified during operational testing included problems with the starter and electrical systems, which were poorly designed and needed to be replaced with military grade components; a removable governor was requested to prevent the engine from running at excessively high speeds and causing damage; and stainless steel exhaust manifolds were needed for maximum durability and to improve silencing capabilities.[19] Phase I and II testing also revealed that accurate gun fire could be delivered at targets up to 200 yards away while an airboat was moving, so a modified MG mount was requested to be installed on the bow of the Aircat.[20]

The first twenty Aircat airboats arrived by military aircraft to Saigon and were delivered to the 5th SF Group (ABN) in the Mekong Delta on 2 October 1966 by a Navy Landing Ship, Tank (LST). The remaining airboats of the initial Hurricane contract were shipped to Vietnam by commercial vessel.[21] Upon delivery, SF Airboat Teams were quickly organized and trained. The standard crew consisted of a boat commander/driver, radio operator, machine gunner, and two rifleman.[22] Airboat SOPs were developed using tactics learned during the operational testing period. Airboats were particularly effective when employed as an element of a coordinated offensive operation.[23] However, lack of any factory installed communications equipment on the boats prevented any coordination to block-off the enemy's withdrawal. Walkie-talkies or backpack radios were often

An Aircat airboat being used by the 199th LIB during Operation Tong Thang II, 20–21 July 1968. Airboats could operate in open water with as many as twelve soldiers aboard. However, all of the extra weight reduced maneuverability and restricted operations in shallow inundated areas. During Phase I testing in December 1964, an Aircat airboat with eleven ARVN Soldiers on board was swamped by water and sank in the Mekong River. Five soldiers drowned. Eye-witnesses accounts suggested that the large number of occupants onboard contributed to the accident.[24] (NARA)

used to communicate, but airboats had to slow down to idle speed in order to receive any incoming radio traffic–high engine noise and interference completely whipped-out any audible radio signals. Transmissions between airboats were usually not received, but other stations in the vicinity could hear outgoing airboat messages very clearly. Airboat radio operators frequently used padded headsets or helmets with built in speakers to alleviate any missed communications.[25]

The Aircat airboat was also issued to conventional forces in Vietnam and was a valuable asset to commanders fighting in a riverine environment. The Aircat was used effectively for patrolling, security, pursuing and intercepting VC watercraft, performing reconnaissance missions similar to vehicle mounted scout platoons, performing resupply and medical evacuations, transporting reserves, and serving as a command utility vehicle.[26] The versatile airboat could also be used in conjunction with ACVs and helicopters for coordinated assaults, and provided rapid mobility on the battlefield.

	Skimmer	**Aircat**
Length -	17 feet	17 feet
Beam -	6 feet 6 inches	7 feet 3 inches
Weight (approx) -	1,200 pounds	1,150 pounds
Composition of Hull -	fiberglass over 3/8"plywood	5 layers molded fiberglass
Shape of Hull -	semi-V bottom	semi-catamaran
Controls -	twin-rudder, steering wheel	twin-rudder, stick
Motor -	0-360 Lycoming, 180 HP	0-360 Lycoming, 180 HP
Speed on waterways -	42 MPR	38 MPR
Steering at high speed -	Excellent	Excellent
Maneuverability at high speed -	Satisfactory	Excellent
Steering at low speed -	Difficult	Difficult
Maximum load -	1,200 pounds	1,000 pounds

A 199th LIB airboat stops to destroy a makeshift VC footbridge constructed from Nippa Palm during Operation Tong Thang II, 20–21 July 1968. A deadly tactic that the VC liked to use was attaching a trip wire to a grenade or claymore mine and when an airboat touched the wire the explosive device would detonate. This type of weapon was only effective if an airboat was stationary or going less than 25 MPR because speeding airboats could often outrun shrapnel.[27] (NARA)

Soldiers of 3rd Platoon, Company D, 5th BN, 199th LIB patrol in Aircat airboats during Operation Tong Thang II, 20–21 July 1968. A favorite Airboat Platoon tactic was to recon an area during the day and then go back out at night to the same location in groups of five-six boats and set up an ambush. Although the Airboats were very loud, the enemy could not pin-point their exact location unless they had visual contact because the sound seemed to come from every direction. (NARA)

A 199th LIB airboat during Operation Tong Thang II, 20–21 July 1968. The Aircat didn't have any passenger seats installed, so soldiers normally sat on the gas tanks, fiberglass sides of the boat, and on the floor. Sitting on the gas tanks caused them to rupture, so many were covered with fiberglass to make them more sturdy and alleviate this type of damage.[28] (NARA)

Echo Company, 15th Engineer BN, 9th ID, was a bridge construction company that had an Airboat Platoon assigned. Mounted on the bow was a gun mount that could fit either a .50 Caliber or 7.62 mm MG. Later, it was determined that firing a .50 Caliber from an airboat was impractical because the gun and its ammunition added too much weight and reduced the Airboats speed. [29] (USAMHI)

An Aircat airboat and Kenner Ski Barge, assigned to the 3rd BDE, 82nd Airborne (ABN) DIV, in 1969. The Aircat had a lightweight catamaran style fiberglass hull that was filled with foam to make the boat unsinkable. There was no armor installed, so speed was the Airboats only protection. "In fact these boats were so light and thinned skinned that a BB would have an easy time of going through them."[30] (U.S. Army)

Aircat airboats assigned to the 9th ID maneuver over mudflats in 1968. Airboats were designed to operate in both mud and water, so an airboat caught in low tide could easily maneuver away, unlike boats with propellers or jet-pumps that had to be extremely cautious of tidal fluctuations. Soldiers have described the tides in the RSSZ as being so high that trees appeared to be growing right out of the water. When the tides receded, the water disappears into tiny streams of 3–4 meters wide and vast mud flats would appear that smelled of rotting vegetation.[31] (USAMHI)

Aircat airboats of the 9th ID maneuver on-and-off the shoreline during a patrol in 1968. This wet and muddy landscape was an ideal location for airboats. However, they did require a high degree of operator proficiency to prevent them from becoming stuck in the mud.[32] Airboats usually received sniper fire, and most often it was difficult to determine which direction the fire was coming from unless a crewmember actually saw the muzzle flash. The VC also employed a light marine-type mine attached to a bamboo pole as an anti-airboat obstacle.[33] (USAMHI)

A silhouette of a 9th ID Aircat airboat returning to Dong Tam after a patrol in 1968. Airboats usually traveled at speeds over 40 MPR on water, reeds and mud flats, so the enemy had a difficult time shooting at them.[34] (USAMHI)

An airboat assigned to the 9th ID in 1968. Notice the M-60 MG mounted on the bow. The 9th ID established two Airboat platoons, which operated with Royal Thai Army (Queen Cobra Regiment) in the RSSZ.[35] (USAMHI)

South Vietnam, 17 April 1968, an airboat glides through the water near Nha Be, an area that was thought to be used by the enemy to organize attacks on Saigon. Notice the antenna mounts attached to the engine frame. The Aircat did not have an electrical system for radio communications. Some field modifications were made by installing antennas and AN/PRC-25 radios operated with headsets.[36] (Photograph by Bruce McIlhaney, used with permission from the *Stars and Stripes*. © 1968, 2006 *Stars and Stripes*)

August 1968, a 199th LIB Aircat airboat mounting a .50 Caliber MG on the bow arrives at the Y-Bridge in Saigon. The recoil from the .50 Caliber MG could easily capsize an airboat when making a sharp turn at very high speed, so vintage WWII era .30 Caliber MGs or M-60 MGs with less recoil were normally used.[37] (NARA)

An Aircat airboat from the 199th LIB patrols a canal during the Defense of Saigon in 1968. Surface conditions of the water had a great influence on airboat operations in combat. Firing weapons on choppy water usually had more effect on weapons accuracy than speed. Tracers were essential for use on moving watercraft because the bullets could be visually walked into the target rather than trying to precisely aim a weapon on a bouncing boat.[38] (NARA)

An Aircat airboat from the 199th LIB moves slowly along a canal in Ghia Dinh Provence during the Defense of Saigon in 1968. Notice the large sticker affixed on the lower cage. The word "Aircat" was printed inside of a white hurricane symbol. The Aircat had a relatively low silhouette as evident in the photo. (NARA)

An Aircat airboat assigned to the 199th LIB patrols a canal in 1968 during Operation Tong Thang II. The high noise levels associated with airboat operations completely eliminated the element of surprise. Additionally, a large water trail was produced by the propeller that could easily be seen by the enemy from a great distance when operating in open terrain.[39] (NARA)

First Sergeant Thomas Williamson, and SP4 Terry Anderson, Airboat driver of the 199th LIB, uses a manual hand-crank to pump 115/145-octane AVGAS into the fuel tank of their airboat prior to a mission in July 1968. Running airboats at high speed for excessive periods caused serious maintenance problems for the engines. Constant exposure to the elements also deteriorated electrical parts rapidly. Exposure to sunlight caused seals to dry and insulation to rot. Water caused corrosion and components to malfunction, particularly when the boats were used at Nha Be which was close to the sea and the water had a high salt content.[40] (NARA)

An Airboat of the 199th LIB refuels at a FSB during Operation Tong Thang II, 20–21 July 1968. Operation Tong Thang II was designed to prevent attacks against the city of Saigon. Airboats could carry heavy loads, were highly maneuverable, and could operate unrestricted in aquatic grass. This was a great advantage over units patrolling by foot or using motorboats with propellers.[41] (USAMHI)

Soldiers of the 199th LIB question local Vietnamese during an airboat patrol in 1968. During the day, fishing boats and sampans carried rice and other goods along the Mekong waterways and airboats would periodically stop and search the boats for enemy weapons and supplies. At sundown, all movement on the waterways stopped and the local inhabitants would disappear. If anything moved at night, it was considered hostile and could be fired upon at will.[42] (USAMHI)

An Airboat from the 199th LIB makes an erratic maneuver during a patrol in 1968. Airboats are steered by vertical rudders, just like an aircraft, but they do not have any breaks and cannot travel in reverse–driving an airboat requires very good operator training and skill.[43] (USAMHI)

The driver's seat on the Aircat was molded hard plastic, and it had a control panel attached to the right side. On the left side was a control stick that operated the fins to turn the boat left or right. On both sides of the driver's seat were two self-sealing twenty-gallon fuel tanks. [44] (NARA)

Cau Lanh, South Vietnam, April 1970. Members of Detachment A-404, Company D, 5th SF Group (ABN) and members of the Vietnamese Mobile Strike Force (MIKE Force) prepare their airboats for an operation in IV CTZ. Notice the individual wearing the coveralls standing on the bank. He is one of four Filipino aircraft mechanics that were contracted to provide 2nd and 3rd echelon maintenance support for the Aircat engines. [45] (NARA)

Two Hurricane Aircats at Camp Boyd in 1970. Camp Boyd was an airboat facility operated by Detachment A-404, 5th SF Group (ABN). Booby traps were a major threat for airboat crews. The VC would tie piano wire between the poles that held fishing traps. When an airboat hit the wire at full speed, there was no warning and it would severely injure or decapitate anyone in the boat. To defeat this menace a large piece of angle iron was welded to the forward gun mount as seen in this photograph. This piece of iron was tall enough to cut the piano wire and protect anyone who was standing or sitting in the boat.[46] (Don Valkie)

An Aircat airboat from the 5th SF Group (ABN). In October 1966, thirty airboats were sent to Can Tho for use during the monsoon season in the Mekong Delta. SFC David Barker is driving the Airboat and instructs his South Vietnamese counterparts on proper waterborne tactics. Airboats made great night ambush platforms–by switching off the engines and drifting with the current airboats could hide inside of the vegetation growing along the riverbanks, and were virtually undetectable. (NARA)

An Aircat on display at the War Memorial of Korea. Notice the cowling that covers the engine and the unique camouflage scheme applied to the boat. This particular airboat was operated by "Blue Dragons" Republic of Korea (R.O.K.) Marine Corps in Vietnam. (MAJ Mandy MacWhirter)

Many Aircats in Vietnam came with a factory sticker affixed on both sides of the boat. Notice the cat claw on the bottom of the letter "A." (John Carrico)

Two examples of identification and crew art that was painted on the rudders of Aircat airboats in Vietnam. El Cid, or "the master," was a 10th century Castilian Knight. SF Mike Force units painted their distinctive skull and crossbones insignia and some airboat crews painted colorful designs. (John Carrico)

Chapter Six

WATER MULES

Two broad categories of boats were required to operate on the extensive canal and river systems in South Vietnam. The Army needed small boats for patrol operations and other boats were required for utility and transport functions. Patrol operations demanded boats with highly maneuverable and sturdy hulls. Utility transport duties required boats with flat and stable decks. Army engineer units were equipped with heavy-duty work boats to erect bridges and pontoons. Combat troops also needed small inflatable boats that could easily be carried in the field and be quickly put into operation for crossing rivers and streams. The Army had some small inflatable landing boats in its inventory but had to turn to the commercial boat industry to find suitable utility craft.

Ski Boats

The Headquarters, United States Army Vietnam (USARV), tasked the Army Concept Team in Vietnam (ACTIVN) to evaluate replacing the BW with a low-cost alternative patrol craft. On 1 October 1967, the AMERI-CAL Division received two commercial pleasure boats to test that were originally designed to tow water skiers. The sixteen foot Tarpon II and twenty foot Marlin III was built by The Kenner Boat Company in Knoxville, Arkansas. The Kenner Ski Barges were sometimes incorrectly referred to as "Boston Whalers," but they were larger, wider, and much cheaper to produce. The Kenner Ski Barge (KSB) had a laminated fiberglass hull, distinctive aluminum handrails, a centerline-aft control station, and was powered by single or twin 80/85-hp outboard motors.[1]

A KSB assigned to the 1st Engineer BN, 1st ID patrols the Saigon River in 1970. The light fiberglass sides of the KSB had a tendency to vibrate at high speeds and would ride better in the water when carrying heavy loads. The smaller Tarpon II required splitting up infantry squads for movement. The larger Marlin III could carry an entire squad plus extra radios, grenadier, and a patrol officer.[2] (NARA)

Tests were conducted between the KSB and the BW at various speeds and different load weights under actual combat conditions at the mouth of the Tra Bong River near Chu Lai. The tests were observed by members from the 9th ID, 196th LIB, 198th LIB, and the U.S. Coast Guard. Both Ski Barge versions could operate at speeds of 25-35 MPR on slightly choppy water, but the flat hulls tended to slap hard on the waves. The Tarpon II could carry seven soldiers (including the coxswain) without affecting performance, and the Marlin III could accommodate up to eleven fully equipped combat infantrymen. Both models could carry three litters on their flat decks, turn 360 degrees in their own length, and were highly maneuverable on calm water. The self-bailing deck was above the waterline and was considered unsinkable because the space between the bottom hull and deck was filled with foam flotation. The Ski Barge had a tendency for water to enter at the transom when executing sharp turns or when stopping abruptly. This could be avoided if the coxswain decelerated when making turns. It was also apparent during the test that the KSB required more skill and extensive training than operating a BW.[3]

Tests concluded that BWs were far more seaworthy and more suited for patrol duties then the KSB. Therefore, it was recommended to use the ski barges strictly for administrative and logistical transport duties in semi-secure areas and not for combat patrolling. Consequently, the KSB did have more usable deck space, was unencumbered by seats, and had a more shallow draft then the BW. The hand rails on both boats usually broke under the weight of heavily laden infantrymen going over the sides. Flaking and chipped paint common to fiberglass hulls was not overly excessive. The construction of the Kenner hull was considered flimsy when compared to the more solidly constructed BW. The Marlin III was better than the Tarpon II for carrying troops and could fit an entire infantry squad. The KSB was not accepted by the 9th ID for MRF operations because they preferred the more agile BW. Overall, the KSB was not considered an effective patrol craft. The ACTIVN Evaluation Team recommended to USARV that the KSB should be used as a utility boat in conjunction with the BW.[4]

Kenner Ski Barge

	16' Tarpon II	20' Marlin III
Length -	15 feet 10 inches	19 feet 8 inches
Beam -	77 inches	94 inches
Draft -	18 inches	18 inches
Max Capacity -	2,000 lbs	3,000 lbs
Weight -	510 lbs	870 lbs
Max Speed -	40 MPH	40 MPH
Material -	Fiberglass	Fiberglass
Transom Height -	20.25 inches	19.5 inches
Fuel Capacity -	18 gallons	18 gallons
Cost -	$895	$1,395

A KSB is being used by soldiers from the 3rd BDE, 82nd ABN DIV to inspect local water traffic near Saigon in 1969. Barely visible behind the paratrooper is a M-60 MG pedestal mount. This was installed based on recommendations from ACTIV during operational testing that occurred in 1967.[5] (U.S. Army)

Soldiers from the 1st Engineer BN, 1st ID, inspect a Vietnamese Sampan on the Saigon River on 6 February 1970. Maintenance problems were encountered with the Johnson 80-hp Engines, such as plug fouling due to excessive oil-to-fuel mixture, which was normally caused by inexperienced operators. Initially, the ski barges were powered by a single 80-hp Johnson Outboard Motor. Later versions of the KSB had twin outboard motors installed.[6] (NARA)

A KSB operated by soldiers from the 1st Engineer BN, 1st ID, on the Saigon River on 6 February 1970. The KSB had a low silhouette and was highly maneuverable. The M-60 MG pedestal mount on the bow had three support legs to keep the gun steady and prevent damage to the hull while firing. (NARA)

KSBs from the 1st Engineer BN, 1st ID, tie up to a resupply point along the Saigon River on 7 February 1970. The KSB was typically used as a utility craft and troop transport because the light construction of the hull made it unsuitable for patrol operations. The KSB could also be used as a medical evacuation craft, radio relay station, and a waterborne observation post utilizing Ground Surveillance Radar (GSR).[7] (NARA)

Soldiers from the 1st Engineer BN, 1st ID, secure KSBs at a resupply point on the Saigon River, 7 February 1970. Notice the distinctive aluminum hand-rails that frequently broke and the flat decks that could carry a lot of gear. (NARA)

Soldiers from the 1st Engineer BN, 1st ID, stop at a resupply point on the Saigon River on 7 February 1970. The initial KSBs did not have any factory installed seats, so soldiers would jury-rig seats using cases of C-Rations. Later models of the KSB came with aluminum seats that could also stow gear underneath. (NARA)

Bridge Erection Boats

The 27-foot aluminum Bridge Erection Boat (BEB) was used by Army engineer units in Vietnam to maneuver components of floating bridges. The BEB was also used to propel rafts, support diving operations, assist in maritime construction projects, transport troops and cargo, and sometimes to patrol inland waterways. The HICE-27D BEB was manufactured by the Aluminum Company of America and was designed to break apart at the center. The front assembly contained an open cockpit that was large enough to carry up to 2,400 lbs of construction equipment and personnel. It also had two large push knees that attached to the bow in order to move bridge components around on the water. The rear section contained the coxswain station and two-three cylinder inboard Detroit Diesel Engines. The engines were connected to transmissions and propeller shafts. The propellers were protected by large skegs and the boat was navigated by a steering wheel attached to rudders. Each section was transported independently in its own cradle and was coupled together after lowering them into the water.[8]

Engineer boat operations in Vietnam were sometimes limited because many units did not have the required number of boats on hand or they were non-operational. Additionally, engineer units lacked boat operators skilled in their MOS. This was mainly because bridge specialists were running convoys with their bridge trucks more often than actually building bridges. It was also found that engineer personnel assigned to combat units were poorly trained. The only course in the U.S. Army that provided formal instruction on the 27-foot BEB was located at the Seventh Army Engineer School in West Germany. If an engineer unit did not have any soldiers who attended the three-week Seventh Army Course, they would have to be given on-the job-training (OJT) in Vietnam. What usually happened was a light-truck driver was given the additional duty of power boat operator verses using a school-trained bridge specialist. This was rather impractical, so the Department of the Army was asked to ensure that engineer bridge specialists were properly trained in the operation and maintenance of the 27-foot BEB before reporting for duty in Vietnam.[9]

The HICE-27D BEB was considered adequate for bridge construction. However, its top speed of only six MPR and maximum range of thirty-six miles limited its usefulness. Post-Vietnam BEBs were equipped with water-jet drives which increased its speed and maneuverability.

A 27-foot, HICE-27D BEB assigned to the 31st Engineers moves down a river toward the village of Song Me in August 1970. These boats were designed to push bridge sections into position using large vertical bumpers called "push knees." The BEB was also used to keep assembled bridges in position against strong river currents. (NARA)

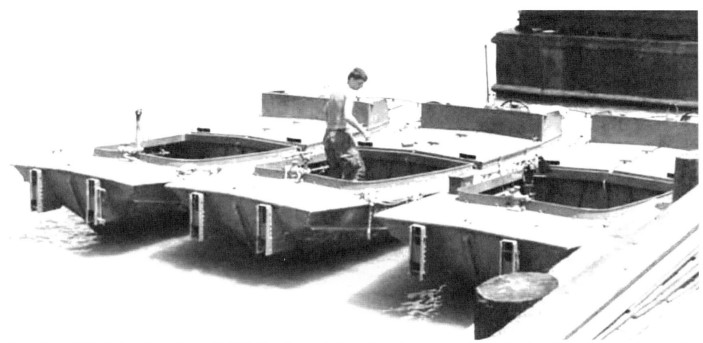

Three Army BEBs tied up to a pier in III CTZ. Here the push knees have been removed from the bow. The aluminum bow section weighed 1,500 lbs and the aft section weighed 6,000 lbs. (Thomas Wonsiewicz)

Soldiers from the 3rd BDE, 82nd ABN DIV, are using a HICE-27D BEB to cross a river in III CTZ. The BEB was a versatile craft that could be used for many different tasks and could carry up to 3,400 lbs of cargo. (NARA)

Engineer Assault Boats

Engineer units in Vietnam also used a heavy-duty work boat to construct bridges and fortifications along the Vietnamese rivers. These boats were cumbersome and originally made for light cargo transport and were also used as pontoons for floating bridges. The Engineer Assault Boat (EAB) was powered by a single 25-hp Chrysler Outboard Motor. When fully loaded with cargo or a squad of combat infantrymen, the EAB barely skimmed the water. When involved in prolonged running on the rivers, the engine covers would have to be removed to prevent overheating. Later, the undependable 25-hp outboard motor was replaced by 40-hp Johnson motor, which greatly improved speed and mobility.[10] The EAB was also used by SF units operating in the Mekong Delta and by some infantry units that did not have organic boats to conduct local river patrols or raids. Problems with the EAB developed when assigning ad-hoc boat operators, who were usually unfamiliar with maintenance procedures of the motors. Also, SF teams in Vietnam had little or no experience using boats during tactical waterborne operations and required some type of formal training.[11]

The EAB was difficult to maintain and operate. The outboard propellers were constantly being tangled in aquatic grass and debris, engine shear pins broke easily, and the utter lack of speed and maneuverability caused assault boat operations to be mostly ineffective.[12] The EAB often ran out of fuel, so at least four-five gallon gas cans were required to be carried on the boats to avoid emergency refueling by helicopters. SF Teams operating the EAB also expressed dissatisfaction about the outboard motors not coming with a basic load of spare parts, most specifically spark plugs and shear pins. Because of a lack of spare sheer pins, sometimes nails were used as a field expedient fix. However, nails did not have the correct tensile strength, and consequently risked further damage to the motors.[13]

Although the EAB was not an agile craft, it did serve its purpose as a work horse in South Vietnam. SF units also conducted some experiments with the EAB by turning them into firing platforms for 81-mm mortars, which was found to be marginally effective.[14]

Soldiers from Company C, 2nd BN, 169th LIB, use an EAB to search huts along the Song An Tan River near Quang Tri on 7 October 1967. This EAB is using a 40-hp outboard motor. Even though this is a B&W photograph, you can still see lots of debris floating in the water which typically fouled outboard propellers. (NARA)

Soldiers try to start a stubborn Johnson 40-hp outboard motor attached to an EAB in 1968. Of special interest is the handrail that ran along the upper-outside edge of the boat and the ribbed aluminum floor. (NARA)

Two EABs move two squads of infantry from the 199th LIB and soldiers from the ARVN 33rd Ranger BN during Operation Shelby, 24 KM west of Saigon, 21–22 August 1967. The EAB was originally made for light cargo transport and also used as pontoons for floating bridges. (NARA)

ENDNOTES

Chapter One – Army Riverine Operations

[1] Funderburk, Raymond E. MAJ "The Delta." *Octofoil, 9th Infantry Division in Vietnam* (Vol.1 /Apr-May-Jun / No. 2). Tokyo, Japan: Dai Nippon Printing Co., Ltd., [c. 1968]: pages 35–36.

[2] *Operational Report of the 9th Infantry Division for period ending 31 January 1968.* Declassified MACV Command Historians Collection. (USAMHI).

[3-4] Richard E. Killblane, *Army Riverine Operations in Vietnam and Panama* (unpublished): pages 1-2.

[5] Funderburk: page 37.

[6] FMFM 8-4, *USMC Doctrine for Riverine Operations.* Washington, D.C.: Department of the Navy, 13 February 1967: page 196.

[7-8] Killblane: page 1-2.

[9] Baker, John W., LTC, and Dickson, Lee C., LTC. "Army Forces in Riverine Operations." *Military Review*, August 1967: page 69.

[10] Friedman, Norman. "Vietnam: The Riverine Force." *U.S. Small Combatants; Including PT Boats, Subchasers, and the Brown Water Navy* Annapolis, Maryland: USNI, 1987: page 357.

[11] Kennedy, James D., LTC, and Dryer, John B., CPT: *Airboats.* Army Concept Team in Vietnam. APO San Francisco 96243: Department of the Army, 15 April 1966: page 1.

[12] FMFM 8-4: page 172.

[13] Henkel, Gerald. SP4 "Sampan Shakedown."*Uptight Magazine*. United States Army Vietnam (USARV) publication, Summer 1968: page 15.

[14] Funderburk: page 37.

[15] Baker: page 69.

[16] Friedman: page 357.

Chapter Two – Mike Boats

[1] U.S. Army Transportation Museum. "River & Canal Transportation." (online).

[2] Killblane: page 3.

[3] Killblane: page 2.

[4] Killblane: page 5.

[5] Killblane: page 7.

[6] Killblane: page 18.

[7] Killblane: page 1-2.

[8] Killblane: page 17.

[9] MACV Command Historians Collection.

[10] Killblane: page 11.

[11] U.S. Army Transportation Museum. "River & Canal Transportation." (online).

[12] *Operational Report and Lessons Learned, Period Ending 31 July 1967,* Headquarters, 9th Infantry Division, APO San Francisco 96370: Department of the Army, 17 January 1968: page 105.

[13] Killblane: page 5.

[14] Killblane: page 4.

[15] *Operational Report and Lessons Learned, Period Ending 31 July 1967,* Headquarters, 9th Infantry Division, APO San Francisco 96370: Department of the Army, 17 January 1968: page 105.

[16] MACV Command Historians Collection.

Chapter Three – Mekong Monsters

[1] U.S. Army Transportation Museum. "Air Cushion Vehicle (ACV) SK-5" (online).

[2] Keaveney, Kevin CPT. "Cavalry Afloat: The 39th Cavalry Platoon in the Mekong Delta." *Armor Magazine*, July–August 1993: page 14.

[3] Vietnam Magazine, October 1998: page 20.

[4] McLeavy, Roy. *Jane's Surface Skimmer Systems* (first edition) 1967–68, McGraw-Hill Company, NY, 1967: page 37.

[5] Hay, John H. Jr. LG. Vietnam Studies: *Tactical and Materiel Innovations.* Washington, D.C.: Department of the Army, 1974: pages 76–77.

[6] Fisher, Robert F. "Air Cushioned Vehicle Unit (Provisional)" (online).

[7] ACV SK-5 (online).

[8] McLeavy: page 37.

[9] Moore, David G., Trip Report – *SK-5 Air Cushion Vehicle.* Army Combat Development Command, APO San Francisco 96375, DoD, 15 August 1968: page 10.

[10] Fisher (online).

[11] Moore: page 3.

[12] Keaveney: page 19.

[13] Moore: page 3.

[14] ACV SK-5 (online).

[15] Moore: page 12.

[16] McLeavy: page 14.

[17] Harlem, Pete., Mil-Mod "Olive Drab" (online).

[18] Keaveney: page 13.

[19] Moore: pages 15–17.

[20] ACV SK-5 (online).

[21] Fisher (online).

[22] Keaveney: page 18.

[23] ACV SK-5 (online).

[24] McLeavy: page 37.

[25] Moore: page 4.

[26] Moore: page 11.

[27-28] Keaveney: page 13.

[29] Moore: enclosure 1 (ACV Firepower).

[30] Keaveney: page 13.

[31-32] Moore: page 4.

[33] Fisher (online).

[34] Keaveney: page 19.

[35] Keaveney: page 14.

[36] Moore: enclosure 3 (After Action Report 1–5 July 1968).

[37] Keaveney: pages 13–14.

[38] Keaveney: page 14 & Wikipedia People Sniffer (online).

[39] Moore: page 6.

[40] Keaveney: page 14.

[41] Moore: enclosure 3.

[42] Keaveney: page 14.

[43] Moore: enclosure 3.

[44] Moore: enclosure 1.

[45] Keaveney: page 37.

[46] Keaveney: page 17.

[47] Keaveney: page 14.

[48] Moore: page 8.

[49] Moore: enclosure 3.

[50] Moore: page 4.

[51] Keaveney: page 13.

[52] Keaveney: page 14 & Wikipedia XM5/M5 Helicopter Armament Subsystem (online).

[53] Moore: enclosure 3.

[54] Moore: page 16.

[55] Fisher (online).

Chapter Four – Fantastic Plastics

[1] U.S. Army Transportation Museum. "Ports – Vietnam." (online).

[2] Richard E. Killblane, *Army Riverine Operations in Vietnam and Panama* (unpublished): page 1.

[3] 720th MP BN Reunion Association History Project. "The Boats of the 720th ~ 1967 to 1970" (online).

[4] Military Police Journal. "MPs' Make Waves" Department of the Army, December 1968: page 11.

[5] U.S. Army Transportation Museum. "458th Transportation Company (Patrol Boat, River)" (online).

[6] Military Police Journal: page 11.

[7] Weddington, David H., LTC, *Military Police River/Harbor Security Company*, Army Concept Team in Vietnam, APO San Francisco 96384; Department of the Army, December 1971.: page I-5.

[8] Weddington: page I-1.

[9] 458th TC (PBR) (online).

[10] Weddington: page ii.

[11] 458th TC (PBR) (online).

[12] Military Police Journal: page 12.

[13] 458th TC (PBR) (online).

[14] Weddington: page II-1.

[15] Email to author from Jerry Wallace, 7 Dec 2010.

[16] Army PBR J-7844 (online).

[17] Sherwood, John D. Dr., Armed With Science. "Papa, Bravo, Romeo: The PBR Story" (online).

[18] Weddington: page I-1.

[19] 458th TC (PBR) (online).

[20] Weddington: page I-1.

[21] Weddington: page I-3.

[22] Weddington: page II-33.

[23] Weddington: page I-3.

[24] Weddington: page II-41.

[25] Weddington: page II-39.

[26] Weddington: page II-41.

[27] Weddington: page II-81.

[28] Weddington: page II-46.

[29] Weddington: pages II-41–42.

[30] Weddington: page II-8.

[31] Weddington: pages II-41–42.

[32] Weddington: pages II-35.

[33] Weddington: page II-86.

[34] Weddington: page II-36.

[35] Weddington: page II-58.

[36] Weddington: page II-70.

[37] Weddington: page II-34.

[38-39] Weddington: page II-63.

[40] Weddington: page II-33.

[41] Weddington: page II-27.

[42] Wonsiewicz, Thomas J., *Reflections of the 458th Transportation Company (PBR)*, November 2003: page 30.

[43] Weddington: page II-33.

[44-45] Boating World Detroit Diesel 6V53N Forum (online).

[46] Weddington: page II-34.

[47] Military Police Journal: page 12.

[48] Weddington: page II-37.

[49] Military Police Journal: page 12.

[50] Weddington: page II-39.

[51] Weddington: page II-2.

[52] Weddington: page II-39.

[53] Weddington: pages I-3–I-4.

[54] Friedman, Norman. "Vietnam Beginnings" *U.S. Small Combatants; Including PT Boats, Subchasers, and the Brown Water Navy* Annapolis, Maryland: USNI, 1987: page 295.

[55] 720th MP BN (online).

[56] Weddington: page I-3.

[57] Wikipedia "Boston Whaler" (online).

[58] Weddington: pages I-3–I-4.

[59] Weddington: page II-48.

[60] Friedman: page 295.

[61] O'Callaghan, Paul., *Kenner Ski Barge*, Army Concept Team in Vietnam, APO San Francisco 96384; Department of the Army, October 1967. Page 3-3.

[62] Weddington: page III-1.

[63] Weddington: page II-51.

[64] Weddington: page II-86.

[65] Weddington: page II-70.

[66] Weddington: page II-66.

[67] *MACV Command History 1970, Volume IV Index*. Declassified MACV Command Historians Collection., 17 April 1971: pages H-34, H-36.

[68] Weddington: page III-2.

[69] Weddington: page II-48.

[70] Wikipedia "Chieu Hoi" (online).

[71] Wikipedia "Kit Carson Scout" (online).

[72] Weddington: page II-48.

Chapter Five – Airboats

[1] Kennedy, James D., LTC, and Dryer, John B., CPT: *Airboats*. Army Concept Team in Vietnam. APO San Francisco 96243: Department of the Army, 15 April 1966: Page 1.

[2] Wollner, James P. *The Bamboo Shoot – The Story of the 2nd Airboat Platoon*., Xlibris Corporation, 2007: Page 75.

[3] Associated Press. "Florida Airboats Tried in Vietnam", Washington D.C., 11 October 1964.

[4-5] Kennedy & Dryer: Page 2.

[6] Kennedy & Dryer: Page 20.

[7] Kennedy & Dryer: Page 23.

[8] FMFM 8-4, *USMC Doctrine for Riverine Operations.* Washington, D.C.: Department of the Navy, 13 February 1967: Page 200.

[9] Wooden Propeller Forum (online).

[10] Wikipedia "Airboat" (online).

[11] Wollner: Page 38.

[12] Kennedy & Dryer: Annex B-3.

[13] Kennedy & Dryer: Page 23.

[14] Kennedy & Dryer: Page 22.

[15] Kennedy & Dryer: Page 23.

[16] Kennedy & Dryer: Page 10.

[17] Wollner: Page 35.

[18] Asente, James., MAJ: *Special Forces Airboat Program.* Enclosure 15 to Operational Report for quarterly period ending on 31 January 1967. Company D, 5th Special Forces Group (Airborne), 1st Special Forces, APO San Francisco 96215, Department of the Army, 9 May 1967: Page 15-2.

[19] Asente: Page 15-1-1.

[20] Kennedy & Dryer: Page 9.

[21] Asente: Page 15-2.

[22] Kennedy & Dryer: Page 6.

[23] Asente: Page 15-2.

[24] Kennedy & Dryer: Page 6.

[25] Kennedy & Dryer: Page 19.

[26] Asente: Page 15-4-1.

[27] Wollner: Page 35.

[28] Kennedy & Dryer: Page 23.

[29-30] Wollner: Pages 67–68.

[31] Wollner: Page 75.

[32] Kennedy & Dryer: Page 10.

[33] Wollner: Page 69.

[34] Kennedy & Dryer: Page 17.

[35] Wollner: Page 77.

[36] Kennedy & Dryer: Annex F-4.

[37] Wollner: Pages 67–68.

[38] Kennedy & Dryer: Page 9.

[39] Kennedy & Dryer: Page 21.

[40] Kennedy & Dryer: Page 23.

[41] Asente: Page 15-4-1.

[42] Wollner: Page 76.

[43] Wikipedia "Airboat" (online).

[44] Wollner: Pages 67–68.

[45] Asente: Page 15-6-1.

[46] Wollner: Pages 34–35.

[47] Wollner: Pages 67–68.

Chapter Six – Water Mules

[1] O'Callaghan, Paul., *Kenner Ski Barge,* Army Concept Team in Vietnam, APO San Francisco 96384; Department of the Army, October 1967: Pages 1-4.

[2] O'Callaghan: Page 1-2.

[3-6] O'Callaghan: Pages 1-4.

[7] OCallaghan: Page 3-2.

[8] *Operator and Organizational Maintenance Manual, Boat, Bridge Erection; Inboard Diesel Engine; Aluminum Hull; Aluminum Company of America, HICE-27D, TM 5-1940-221-12.* Washington, D.C.: Department of the Army, June 1974: Page I-1.

[9] *Operational Report - Lessons Learned, Period Ending 30 April 1968.* Engineer Headquarters, 79th Group (Construction), APO 96491: Department of the Army, 15 August 1968: Page 24.

[10] 720th MP BN Reunion Association History Project. "The Boats of the 720th ~ 1967 to 1970" (online).

[11] *Flood After Action Report.* Detachment B-41, 5th Special Forces Group (Airborne), lst Special Forces, APO 09215, Department of the Army, 27 November 1966: Page 13-7.

[12] Flood: Page 13-9.

[13] Flood: Page 13-16.

[14] Flood: Page 13-17.

BIBLIOGRAPHY

Published Sources

Associated Press. "Florida Airboats Tried in Vietnam", Washington D.C., 11 October 1964.

Baker, John W., LTC, and Dickson, Lee C., LTC. "Army Forces in Riverine Operations." *Military Review*, August 1967.

Friedman, Norman. *U.S. Small Combatants; Including PT Boats, Subchasers, and the Brown Water Navy* Annapolis, Maryland: United States Naval Institute, 1987.

Keaveney, Kevin CPT. "Cavalry Afloat: The 39th Cavalry Platoon in the Mekong Delta." *Armor Magazine*, July–August 1993.

McLeavey, Roy. *Jane's Surface Skimmer Systems*. First Edition, 1967–68., McGraw-Hill Book Company, New York, 1967.

Wollner, James P. *The Bamboo Shoot – The Story of the 2nd Airboat Platoon.*, Xlibris Corporation, 2007.

Unpublished Sources

Asente, James., MAJ: *Special Forces Airboat Program.* Enclosure 15 to Operational Report for quarterly period ending on 31 January 1967. Company D, 5th Special Forces Group (Airborne), 1st Special Forces, APO San Francisco 96215, Department of the Army, 9 May 1967.

BOATS of the United States Navy; NAVSHIPS 250-452. Washington, D.C.: US GPO, May 1967.

Flood After Action Report. Detachment B-41, 5th Special Forces Group (Airborne), lst Special Forces, APO 09215, Department of the Army, 27 November 1966.

FMFM 8-4, *USMC Doctrine for Riverine Operations.* Washington, D.C.: Department of the Navy, 13 February 1967.

Funderburk, Raymond E. MAJ "The Delta." *Octofoil, 9th Infantry Division in Vietnam* (Vol. 1/Apr-May-Jun/No. 2). Tokyo, Japan: Dai Nippon Printing Co., Ltd., [c.1968].

Hay, John H. Jr. LG. Vietnam Studies: *Tactical and Materiel Innovations.* Washington, D.C.: Department of the Army, 1974.

Henkel, Gerald. SP4 "Sampan Shakedown."*Uptight Magazine.* United States Army Vietnam (USARV) publication, Summer 1968.

Kennedy, James D., LTC, and Dryer, John B., CPT: *Airboats.* Army Concept Team in Vietnam. APO San Francisco 96243: Department of the Army, 15 April 1966.

Killblane, Richard E., *Army Riverine Operations in Vietnam and Panama.*

MACV Command History 1970, Volume IV, Index. Declassified MACV Command Historians Collection, 17 April 1971. (USAMHI).

Military Police Journal. "MPs Make Waves." Department of the Army, December 1968.

Moore, David G., *Trip Report – SK-5 Air Cushion Vehicle*. Army Combat Development Command, APO San Francisco 96375, DoD, 15 August 1968.

Operator and Organizational Maintenance Manual, Boat, Bridge Erection; Inboard Diesel Engine; Aluminum Hull; Aluminum Company of America, HICE-27D, TM 5-1940-221-12. Washington, D.C.: Department of the Army, June 1974.

Operational Report and Lessons Learned, Period Ending 31 July 1967, Headquarters, 9th Infantry Division, APO San Francisco 96370: Department of the Army, 17 January 1968.

Operational Report - Lessons Learned, Period Ending 30 April 1968. Engineer Headquarters, 79th Group (Construction), APO 96491: Department of the Army, 15 August 1968.

Operational Report of the 9th Infantry Division for period ending 31 January 1968. Declassified MACV Command Historians Collection.

O'Callaghan, Paul., *Kenner Ski Barge*, Army Concept Team in Vietnam, APO San Francisco 96384; Department of the Army, October 1967.

Wallace, Jerry., Email to author, 7 Dec 2010.

Weddington, David H., LTC, *Military Police River/Harbor Security Company*, Army Concept Team in Vietnam, APO San Francisco 96384; Department of the Army, December 1971.

Wonsiewicz, Thomas J., *Reflections of the 458th Transportation Company (PBR)*, November 2003.

Online Sources

Fisher, Robert F. "Air Cushioned Vehicle Unit (Provisional)." [4 November 2006]

U.S. Army Transportation Museum. "Air Cushioned Vehicle (ACV) SK-5." [3 November 2006]

U.S. Army Transportation Museum. "River & Canal Transportation." [3 November 2006]

U.S. Army Transportation Museum. "458th Transportation Company (Patrol Boat, River)." [3 November 2006]

U.S. Army Transportation Museum. "Ports – Vietnam." [3 November 2006]

720th MP Bn Reunion Association History Project. "The Boats of the 720th ~ 1967 to 1970." [9 November 2006]

Wikipedia "People Sniffer." [28 November 2010]

Wikipedia "XM5/M5 Armament Subsystem." [28 November 2010]

Harlem, Pete., MILL-MOD "Olive Drab." [28 November 2010]

Sherwood, John D. Dr., Armed With Science. "Papa, Bravo, Romeo: The PBR Story." [5 December 2010]

Wikipedia "Boston Whaler" [12 December 2010]

458th PBR - VUNG RO BAY (1966 - 1970). [12 December 2010]

458th Sea Tigers. [12 December 2010]

Army PBR J-7844 Restoration. [1 January 2011]

Boating World Detroit Diesel 6V53N Forum. [1 January 2011]

Wikipedia "Kit Carson Scouts." [2 January 2011]

Wikipedia "Chieu Hoi." [2 January 2011]

Wikipedia "Airboat." [8 January 2011]

Wooden Propeller Forum. [17 October 2010]

ABOUT THE AUTHOR

John M. Carrico is a twenty-year U.S. Army veteran, who served as an airborne-infantryman until he retired as a Sergeant First Class in 2004. He is currently serving as an Operations Planning Specialist for the United States Army Europe (USAREUR) located in Heidelberg, Germany. John earned his Associate of Arts degree from the University of Maryland in 2004, authored a book titled, *Vietnam Ironclads; A Pictorial History of U.S. Navy River Assault Craft 1966–1970* and produced several documentary films about the Vietnam War. His hobbies include collecting militaria and restoring antique military vehicles.

Made in United States
Orlando, FL
10 January 2023

28540024R00058